To DAVID & MICH[...]

with Love & best wishes

Xmas 1967

Prince Charles
The Future King

Prince Charles
The Future King

Graham & Heather Fisher

W. H. ALLEN
LONDON
1966

© Graham & Heather Fisher Ltd. 1966
Printed and bound in Great Britain by
The Garden City Press Limited
Letchworth, Hertfordshire
for the publishers
W. H. Allen & Company
Essex Street, London, W.C.2

Contents

Illustrations

Foreword

A definitive biography of H.R.H. Charles Philip Arthur George, 21st Prince of Wales, must necessarily wait upon the future. But it is perhaps possible, as he enters upon his years of manhood, to essay an interim portrait. Possible . . . but not easy. His royal parents, until now, have imposed upon themselves a policy of exposing him to public life as little as possible, and few will quarrel with that decision. The selection of his schools—Cheam, Gordonstoun and Timbertop in Australia—has perhaps been influenced, in part at least, by their comparative inaccessibility. His achievements in the classroom and on the playing field have received a minimum of publicity, though sometimes publicity has followed where it was probably neither expected nor desired. Though much has been written about him, little is really known. The picture which emerges is one-sided and certainly incomplete.

In attempting to round the portrait we have, wherever possible, gone to first-hand sources for our information, seeking out and talking with people who have had the opportunity of seeing, meeting or knowing him, however briefly, at varying times in his young life. Even human recollection is fallible, of course, and we have been at pains to check and cross-check as far as possible, sifting the wheat from the chaff, fact from fiction. For instance, we could find no evidence to support the hitherto generally accepted story that, as a child, he was frightened of water. On the contrary, we are assured by someone who should know that almost from babyhood he was completely in his element in the water and looked forward eagerly to his swimming lessons in the Buckingham Palace pool. Most of those with whom we have talked prefer, for perhaps obvious reasons, to remain anonymous. We are nevertheless grateful to them.

G. & H. F.

*For
Linda, Janet
and Brandon*

I   *" It's A Boy ! "*

I

It was a drab, grey Sunday evening in mid-November. The hour was late. But neither the lateness of the hour nor the greyness of the weather had yet served to diminish the waiting crowd which had been growing all day before the tall railings of Buckingham Palace.

Surely, they murmured among themselves as they pressed in on the patrolling sentries and stolidly patient policemen . . . surely it couldn't be long now. Something must happen soon.

In the darkness across the palace forecourt a door on the right of the palace opened and the figure of a man was silhouetted briefly against the light inside the Privy Purse entrance. He hurried across the forecourt, almost breaking into a run in his excitement as he neared the palace railings and the eager, waiting crowd beyond.

As it approached, the figure resolved itself into one of the royal pages wearing the navy-blue battledress style uniform introduced by King George VI as a war-time measure of economy and practicality. It was, in fact, Stanley Childs, a long-time member of the royal staff and today one of the Queen's personal pages. That he was the bearer of important tidings that November night showed plainly in his face.

"It's a boy!" he informed the nearest segment of the waiting crowd . . . an announcement, unofficial though it was, which was greeted by a spontaneous outburst of cheering. The cheers swelled rapidly to a roar as the eagerly-awaited news was passed from mouth to mouth.

But it was not only a boy who was born in Buckingham Palace that November night. It was also a Prince, born in direct succession to the Throne . . . the future King.

In London's Hyde Park, the following morning, a rumbling salute of guns underwrote the fact that the accession to the Throne was assured. The rejoicing echoed around the Commonwealth. In Canada, as soon as the baby's name was known, an arctic outpost was similarly named of Prince Charles Island as a permanent memorial. In Britain, the baby's aunt, Princess Margaret, reportedly quipped that she would undoubtedly be known as 'Charley's aunt' from then on.

By giving birth not only to a bouncing seven pound six ounce baby, but a baby boy at that, the royal mother had more than lived up to the affectionate reputation she had long held in the hearts of the British people. The warm-hearted Cockney who commented, "Good old Liz. We knew she wouldn't let us down," was speaking for everyone.

Her Most Excellent Majesty Elizabeth II, as she now is, was at that time still Princess Elizabeth, Duchess of Edinburgh, twenty-two years of age, and newly married twelve months before to the Duke of Edinburgh, the exiled Greek prince whose blond masculinity seemed somehow to combine film star looks with the well-scrubbed virility of an athlete fresh from the shower.

They had first met some nine years earlier. Princess Elizabeth was then a girl of thirteen and Philip a young naval cadet as yet untried by the fires of war. It was during the war years, with Philip at sea on the bridge of a destroyer and the Princess lodged in the comparative safety of Windsor Castle, that what had started as a simple boy and girl friendship gradually ripened into love. Christmas cards, an exchange of photographs, increasingly affectionate letters . . . for them, as for other young people, these were the links in the chain that led to love. Meetings were rare, and doubly precious on that account . . . like Philip's war-time visit to Windsor where the performance of the principal boy in a home-made pantomime revealed that even a princess may have fetching legs.

Courtship ran the customary course common to all young people in love . . . evening strolls along leafy lanes, country spins in Philip's little sports car, theatre visits and tête-à-tête suppers. Holiday visits to Sandringham and Balmoral brought them closer still. Then came the testing-time of separation, a bitter-sweet four months of parting when the Princess, a photograph of Philip, handsomely bearded in true naval tradition, close beside her on the dressing table in her cabin, visited South Africa with her parents.

Back in Britain, the Princess made no secret of her joy at being reunited with Philip. The happiness in her eyes was plain for all to see. Their wedding, in Westminster Abbey that November, was the first in the Royal Family since the Duke of Kent had married Princess Marina, nearly a quarter-of-a-century before.

The honeymoon over, the newlyweds settled in at Buckingham Palace with the bride's parents while their new home at Clarence House was being renovated and made ready for them. They occupied a small suite at the front of the palace, the same suite which Prince Charles now occupies whenever he is at home.

First news of an impending 'happy event' for the newlyweds came in the June with the announcement that Princess Elizabeth would be undertaking no more public engagements after the end of the month. The British people, long adept at translating such cryptic official announcements, knew what that meant, and the following day, when the Princess went to the Derby, public enthusiasm was such that police had some difficulty in clearing a path through the crowd for her car.

At Buckingham Palace, work was put in hand to renovate the royal nursery which the Princess had once shared with her sister. The cot and baby basket they had both used were brought out of storage and refurbished for use by another generation of royal children. The royal physicians began their succession of calls.

Pregnancy ran its customary course. At Buckingham Palace, the Princess, advised to exercise as much as possible by her doctors, took to walking in the gardens, morning and afternoon, accompanied by her pet corgi, Susan. Prince Philip showed himself a devoted and attentive husband, spending as much time with his young bride as duty permitted. Though the two of them ate occasionally with the King and Queen, whenever possible they had their meals alone in the privacy of their own small suite. At Balmoral, that summer, the Princess was noticeably less active than usual, and, fearful lest it might harm the expected baby, she gave up her favourite pastime of horse riding.

From all parts of the world gifts began to stream in, more woolly bootees and knitted jackets than a single baby could possibly require or ever hope to use. Many were passed on subsequently and without publicity to more needy youngsters.

"Surely," the Princess was reported as commenting on one occasion, "I'm not the only woman who is having a baby."

She wasn't, but the baby she was expecting was the most important to be born into British history for many a year.

Apart from taking additional exercise in the palace gardens and foregoing her customary horse-riding at Balmoral, the Princess departed little from her normal routine. Four days before the baby was born she was out at a private film show; two nights beforehand she went with Prince Philip to dine with Lord and Lady Brabourne at the Mountbatten residence in Chester Street. Lady Brabourne is the daughter of Earl Mountbatten of Burma, Prince Philip's uncle.

The Princess and her husband were returning from this dinner party when they encountered a small group of waiting photographers clustered around the entrance to the palace and the sudden glare of flashbulbs as the car turned into the palace forecourt may have startled the young mother-to-be. Be that as it may, Prince Philip, who was driving the car, was later said to have been both disturbed and displeased by what he regarded as lack of consideration, and his evident and long-standing dislike for photographic lenses can perhaps be traced back to that occasion.

II

It was November 14, 1948. Princess Elizabeth was seen by her doctors in the morning and again towards tea-time. Constantly close at hand throughout the day was her beloved 'Bobo'—Margaret Macdonald—the long-time personal maid who first took charge of her as assistant nanny when she was a baby of only a few weeks and is still with her today.

Early that evening the Princess rode down in the lift to the first floor of the palace and made her way towards the Buhl Room suite, a guest apartment with heavy mahogany furnishings which Prince Philip had occupied when he first moved into the palace for the official announcement of their betrothal. One of the rooms of the suite had been adapted with special lighting and the necessary electrical fittings for surgical apparatus required for the recent operation on the Princess's father, King George VI, and was consequently eminently suited for use as a delivery ward. The Princess awaited the birth of her first child in an adjoining bedroom. Sister Helen Rowe, the royal midwife, had moved into the palace some time previously and Mr. (later Sir) William Gilliatt, the gynaecologist, had been staying there since the previous night. They were joined now by Sir John Weir and Mr. (now Sir) John Peel. Mr. Vernon Hall, the anaesthetist, completed the team for this all-important birth.

After ensuring that his young wife was all right, Prince Philip, who had gone along to the Buhl Room with her, changed into grey flannels and a white sports shirt and went along for an energetic game of squash with Michael Parker, his personal secretary and long-time friend, in the indoor court which adjoins the swimming pool at the rear of the palace. Invigorated by their game of squash, the two young men cooled off with a swim in the pool, and Philip was still shirt-sleeved, chatting with the King and Queen in their sitting room, when news of the baby's birth was brought to them.

It is not difficult to picture the scene, the King shaking his son-in-law warmly by the hand, the Queen Mother (as she now is) embracing him in her affectionate fashion. "Isn't it wonderful," she was heard to say soon afterwards and the remark was perhaps more a statement of grandmotherly joy than a question requiring any answer.

Prince Philip, of course, was considerably elated, as young men experiencing fatherhood for the first time are apt to be. As soon as the doctors would permit, he hurried along to see his wife and the baby, the King and Queen following closely upon his heels. Another visitor for the new-born baby that same night was his great-grandmother, Queen Mary, still regal and erect at eighty-one.

She had been informed by telephone at Marlborough House and had driven straight over. Another telephone call conveyed the news to Princess Margaret, who was staying with the Duke and Duchess of Scarbrough.

Rather after the manner of a conjuror producing a rabbit from a hat, Prince Philip sprang an unexpected surprise in the form of a magnificent bouquet of roses, carnations and freesia as a congratulatory gift for his young wife, and later that night, in the Centre Room which gives on to Buckingham Palace's famous balcony, he was busily pouring champagne for members of the Royal Household and the Royal Family's personal staff.

"Come and wet the baby's head," he called out affably to two members of the staff who chanced to pass by the open doorway.

There was no official witness to the birth of the future King in the person of the Home Secretary . . . an ancient and perhaps embarrassing custom dating back to the distant days of James II and presumably designed to ensure that no changeling was ever introduced into the royal line.

The last time there was any attempt at observing this curious custom was at the birth of Princess Margaret. It proved a considerable fiasco. The Home Secretary of the day, Mr. J. R. Clynes, travelled to Scotland and arrived at Glamis Castle, the family home of the Queen Mother, to find that the royal physicians had been somewhat optimistic in their forecast as to the baby's birth. Days lengthened into a week, then two weeks, with a considerably embarrassed Home Secretary waiting time out at Airlie Castle, some eight miles from Glamis. The summons to Glamis, when it finally reached him, came at somewhat short notice. As a result, the only witnessing he did consisted of no more than a glimpse of the newly-born baby princess peacefully asleep.

Now, with the start of another royal generation, King George VI, viewing this ancient custom as the anachronism it was, had finally decided to end it.

"The attendance of a Minister of the Crown at a birth in the Royal Family is not a statutory requirement or a constitutional necessity," explained the official statement issued for the King. "It is merely the survival of an archaic custom, and the King feels it is unnecessary to continue further a practice for which there is no legal requirement."

Relieved of this embarrassing duty, the Home Secretary waited for news of the future King's birth to be telephoned through to him. Then he filled in the space left for the missing word, 'boy' or 'girl', on the waiting telegrams and so passed the news on to the countries of the Commonwealth and Empire.

It was eleven o'clock that night when the official announcement of the birth, quaintly worded in royal tradition, was posted on the palace railings: "The Princess Elizabeth, Duchess of Edinburgh, was safely delivered of a Prince at 9.14 p.m. today. Her Royal Highness and her son are both doing well."

As news of the baby's birth spread by a form of bush telegraph throughout London, taxis and cars, bringing more and yet more people, began to converge on the open space in front of the palace. Extra police had to be called out to control the traffic and by half-past eleven it was conservatively estimated that a crowd of some eight thousand people was packed tight around the palace railings and on the steps of the Victoria Memorial.

Inside the palace, the switchboard was predictably inundated with telephone calls of congratulations and good wishes. Outside the palace, the growing crowd grew cheerfully noisier, singing and cheering. Shouts of "Good old Liz" and "We want Philip" punctuated this good-natured tumult, but hopes that the baby's father might appear on the balcony went unfulfilled.

Mindful of the fact that the Princess was sleeping at the front of the palace, police officers did their best to stem the noise, though without any noticeable success.

"Stop making that noise and keep quiet," one police officer ordered a section of the crowd, more curtly than diplomatically.

"He's our Prince and we'll cheer him if we like," a chagrined loyalist in the crowd retorted indignantly.

Finally, it took a personal plea from a senior royal official . . . "Please, Princess Elizabeth wants some rest. Prince Philip is with her and there will be nothing more tonight" . . . before the hub-bub began to subside and the crowd was persuaded to melt away.

2   " *That's* Prince *Charles* "

I

The future King was a week old—and fast asleep at the time—when he held his first court, lying cosily in his cradle of peach-coloured satin, fussy with frills of cream net and bows of blue satin, the selfsame cradle that his mother and Aunt Margaret had used as babies, while family friends and members of the royal staff tiptoed quietly by, paying silent homage. All agreed with his mother that he was 'quite adorable'. But in the weeks which followed the royal mother was said to be slightly perturbed when well-meaning people inquired of her how 'the baby' was doing. She felt, as she confided on one occasion, that they should refer to her baby son as 'His Royal Highness'.

For the first month after his birth the baby occupied the dressing room adjoining his mother's bedroom, sleeping in a Moses basket which had been used, in turn, by all royal children since Queen Victoria's day. Family heirlooms carefully treasured since his mother and aunt were children were brought out of storage and put to good use again. The round wicker basket lined with pink silk, which held the baby's things, had done sterling service in the royal nursery before . . . and has done since. As recently as the birth of Prince Edward it was still in use. The small silver box for holding safety pins was another family heirloom. The silver-backed hairbrush with which his mother later fluffed up the downy hair on the baby's head was the same one employed for her own curls in babyhood. The silver rattle Charles was soon to clutch in a chubby fist . . . and the teething ring in which he was to find comfort later . . . these, too, had been handed down from his mother's infancy.

Helen Lightbody—unmarried, but 'Mrs.' by royal tradition—was engaged as the future King's nanny. A Scot from Edinburgh of slender build and upright carriage, Mrs. Lightbody was no stranger to the Royal Family, having previously been nanny to the small sons of the Duke and Duchess of Gloucester, with whom she had frequently visited both Sandringham and Balmoral. To assist Mrs. Lightbody as nurserymaid, the baby's mother hired another Scot, at least by upbringing if not by birth. Mabel Anderson—soon to be affectionately known as 'Mamba' in the royal nursery—a tall, softly-spoken, fresh-complexioned girl in her early twenties, had been born in Lancashire, but reared in Scotland after her policeman father was killed in the blitz on Liverpool.

While Mrs. Lightbody was engaged largely on account of her previous experience with the Gloucesters, Mabel Anderson was Princess Elizabeth's personal choice. The Princess selected her for the job after personally interviewing a number of applicants. The soundness of her choice is demonstrated by the fact that when Mrs. Lightbody left the royal nursery in 1956, when Charles was eight, Mabel Anderson showed herself as more than competent to take over. She is still there today, bringing up Andrew and Edward with the same firm, yet quiet discipline which she once exercised over Prince Charles and his more high-spirited young sister, Princess Anne.

But Anne's birth was still some twenty months in the future that December day when His Royal Highness Charles Philip Arthur George was christened in the white and gold Music Room at Buckingham Palace. The baby's birth had been formally registered earlier that day. Buckingham Palace lies officially within the City of Westminster and so it was the Registrar from Caxton Hall, Mr. J. S. Clare, who attended at the palace and made the necessary entry in the register for Prince Philip to sign.

The christening ceremony was conducted by the Archbishop of Canterbury. The gold lily font had been personally designed by Prince Albert for the christening of Queen Victoria's first child, the christening robe of white silk and Honiton lace dated equally from Victoria's day, and the holy water employed for the ceremony had been brought specially from the River Jordan. The sponsors clustered around the font were headed by King George VI, Queen Mary and Princess Margaret. King Haakon of Norway and Prince George of Greece were represented by proxies. The remaining godparents were the Dowager Marchioness of Milford Haven, the baby's great-aunt on his father's side, the Hon. David Bowes-Lyon, the brother to whom Queen Elizabeth was always so close, and Lady Brabourne, Prince Philip's cousin. No baby could have wished for a more distinguished company.

The baby Prince was only five weeks old when the Royal Family left London that December for their traditional Christmas stay at Sandringham House, their country home in Norfolk. Drawn by the hope of a glimpse of the new baby, more countryfolk than usual gathered at Wolferton station that year to witness the royal arrival, though still not so many that you could term it a crowd. Wolferton is, after all, a fairly isolated spot.

Shawl-wrapped against the Christmas cold, the baby was carried quickly from royal train to royal car. But the car's interior light was considerably left on as it drew out of the station yard so that those who waited should not be disappointed. A small loyal cheer sped the vehicle on its way and inside the car Nanny Lightbody took the baby's hand in her own to give an answering wave of acknowledgement. It was, even if he was too young to understand and it is now too long ago for his memory to recall, Prince Charles' first lesson along the road to monarchy.

II

Princess Elizabeth's first outing after the birth of Prince Charles was a short excursion along the Mall to look over Clarence House, the home of her own she was awaiting so eagerly, though it was to be close on another eight months before the house was in a sufficient state of readiness for her and Prince Philip to move in.

More than a year's work and the expenditure of some £55,000 went into converting this one-time residence of the Duke of Connaught into a fitting home for the royal newlyweds and their baby son. Clarence House, when the Princess saw it first, was in a sad state of dilapidation. Apart from its war-time use as offices for the Red Cross, it had not been lived in for thirty years; not been re-decorated for twenty years before that. War-time bomb damage had done nothing to improve what new amenities the place may have had. There was no bathroom, no electric lighting apart from a few makeshift war-time fittings, and the old-fashioned gas lighting system was in no condition to function even if it had been convenient.

But all that was changed by the time the Princess finally moved in with her husband and baby in July of the following year. The Princess surely beamed a smiling approval as she wandered from room to room of her spacious, modern, labour-saving home, centrally heated and lit by glistening chandeliers, supervising the arranging of the wedding gifts with which it was largely furnished.

The nursery suite was at the front of the building, looking out across the Mall to St. James's Park. With the subsequent birth of Princess Anne, it was extended to a total of five rooms, including its own small kitchen.

Focal point of nursery life was the day nursery, a light, spacious, airy room. Close carpeted and with walls in a pastel tone of duck-egg blue, it was furnished very much as the Princess' own nursery had been in childhood.

Chintz curtains patterned with a design of hoops and parasols and Victorian nursemaids hung at the windows. The pattern was caught and repeated by the high-backed winged armchairs which flanked the fireplace, surrounded by a sturdy fireguard to safeguard small occupants of the nursery from possible harm. There was a matching sofa and also two small easy chairs without arms so that hands and elbows could move freely when the baby was being fed or changed.

An applewood table occupied the centre of the room and against one wall stood a glass-fronted cabinet to hold a growing collection of toys and games, books and knick-knacks. The erection of a folding playpen—the selfsame playpen that was still in use when Prince Edward, in turn, reached the crawling stage some fifteen years later—somewhat congested the available space upon occasion.

Emphasising the fact that this was no ordinary baby was the size of the nursery staff . . . Nanny Lightbody with Mabel Anderson to assist her, a nursery footman to bring food from the kitchen, lay the table, clean shoes and generally fetch and carry, and two housemaids taking it turn and turn about to dust and clean. Later, after the birth of Princess Anne and the subsequent move back to Buckingham Palace, there was a further increase with the engagement of a second nurserymaid, Agnes Cooper.

With the move to Clarence House, that ancient home of Britain's monarchs became part of the traditional round for London's visiting tourists. The real lure, of course, was the ever-present possibility of a fleeting glimpse of the baby Prince as he came and went from his daily outing.

The Queen, as she now is, has always held that abundant fresh air and plenty of light, natural exercise are the basic essentials for a happy, healthy childhood. Now, with the birth of her first child, she had the opportunity to put her theories to the test. Every day, wet or fine, Prince Charles went out of doors for his daily constitutional, initially in the same tall, high-wheeled black baby carriage which his mother had occupied in babyhood and, later, in a rather cumbersome-looking push-chair in which he could sit up and look around at the world at large.

Sometimes these airings were confined to the garden of Clarence House itself, but there were other occasions when the baby and his nanny ventured further afield, to St. James's Park and Green Park. His mother's instructions to whoever accompanied the baby on these outings were crystal clear: individuals who chanced to recognise the baby might be permitted the privilege of a close-up peep, but in no circumstances must a crowd be permitted to gather. She did not want her baby son treated as a film star, the Princess said, firmly. Inevitably, of course, crowds did tend to gather and when this happened the baby's outings were switched to more out-of-the-way locations, such as Richmond Park, where Charles, as he graduated from babyhood to boyhood, had fun stalking the tame deer with a toy gun, shouting "Bang-bang-bang" at the top of a pair of healthy young lungs.

From birth, the baby Prince was subject to the same sort of clockwork timetable which, as Prince of Wales and later as King, will almost assuredly dog him to the end of his days, just as it constantly jogs the elbow of his mother, the Queen, as she tackles the never-ending royal round of ship-launchings and tree-plantings, hospital openings and factory inspections, each with its quota of speeches and handshakes.

Nursery life started promptly at seven o'clock in the morning. A morning wash for the baby Prince was followed by breakfast. Milk from a bottle was succeeded, as the baby grew towards boyhood, by groats and rusks, strained baby foods and then more manly diet. Once he could toddle, Charles wore a denim playsuit for romping about the nursery. For more formal occasions, there were short trousers and tunic blouse.

At nine o'clock Nanny Lightbody would take the baby downstairs to spend half-an-hour with his mother. At half-past ten came the morning outing, with the royal corgis, Susan and Sugar, as additional attendants and a watchful detective never very far away. At twelve o'clock the small procession of baby and nanny, detective and dogs would return to the house for lunch, with the sentry on the gate presenting arms with a flourish and the policeman snapping a smart salute.

Lunch, for Charles, was followed by a nap in the nursery until half-past three. Then it was out into the garden for a further airing . . . or sometimes a trip along the road to see Granny in her more spacious garden at Buckingham Palace. Half-past four was time for afternoon tea. Charles, once he was out of the strictly baby stage, developed a considerable liking for banana sandwiches. These, with jam sandwiches, fairy cakes and a beaker of milk, made up the tea-time meal.

After tea came that period of the day to which Charles, as he grew from babyhood to boyhood, looked forward more than any other. For an all-too-brief hour-and-a-half after tea he and his mother could have each other to themselves. For the Princess it was a welcome opportunity to savour the joys of motherhood to the full, and regal dignity did not prevent her going down on her hands and knees to crawl about the sitting-room carpet as she joined her small son in childhood games involving woolly animals, toy soldiers, building blocks and pull-along trucks.

Increasing royal duties as deputy for her sick father compelled the Princess to be away from home a good deal, visiting Wales, Northern Ireland and the Channel Islands among other places.

But whenever she was free she missed no opportunity of personally taking her baby son back to the nursery at the end of their evening play session and donning a waterproof apron to give him his daily bath.

Prince Philip would often join mother and son in the nursery bathroom on these occasions and the resulting bath session was often uproarious and always very wet, with water flying in all directions. Plastic ducks and toy boats enlivened the bath-time proceedings. Later, too, there was a toy diver which could be made to submerge and then surface again by operating a rubber bulb at the end of a length of flexible tubing. Man-like, Prince Philip scorned the offer of a rubber apron to safeguard his clothes during these watery playtimes and more than once ended up thoroughly soaked, particularly after Princess Anne was born and had grown of an age to join in the fun.

Prince Philip was at this time still in the navy and a few months after the move to Clarence House he journeyed to Malta to take up new duties as first lieutenant aboard the destroyer *Chequers.* With her husband in Malta and her baby son in London, the Princess inevitably found her loyalties divided. Dexterously she compromised, remaining in Britain for Prince Charles' first birthday before flying out to Malta to spend Christmas with her husband, leaving her small son to spend Christmas as usual at Sandringham with his grandparents, the King and Queen.

For the Princess, the wrench of parting was made easier by the knowledge that her mother would be close at hand to keep a grandmotherly eye on Prince Charles. This comforting knowledge was to stand her in good stead in the years ahead, the years which followed her father's death, though that fact and its accompanying sadness was mercifully hidden from her during these happy early years of marriage and motherhood.

Some few years later, during the long round-the-world tour which followed her father's death and her own accession to the Throne, the Queen, as she had then become, was asked in Australia if she did not miss her children when she was away from them.

"More than they miss us, I'm afraid," she replied, with a wry smile. "You see, they have a doting grandmother."

The Princess was again in Malta with Prince Philip for her birthday the following April, an occasion rendered doubly pleasurable to them both through the knowledge that Prince Charles was soon to have a small playmate in the royal nursery, a secret the world was to share shortly afterwards when it was again announced that the Princess would be undertaking "no further public engagements".

III

The future King was one year and nine months old when his younger sister, Princess Anne, was born at Clarence House on August 15, 1950. Prince Philip, newly promoted to the rank of lieutenant-commander with the frigate *Magpie* as his first command, was home on leave from the Navy. He was, in fact, posing for a miniature of himself which he was having painted as a gift for his wife, when a telephone call giving news of the baby's birth brought the sitting to an early end. Once again, he celebrated fatherhood by ordering champagne all round and personally pouring it out for the Clarence House staff. Prince Charles made an early and fleeting public appearance when, attracted by the excitement of the big crowd outside Clarence House, he asked to be lifted up to a window so that he could see what was going on. People in the crowd, spotting the small, sturdy figure at the window, began to wave. Excitedly Charles waved back.

For the royal mother, the birth of the six-pound Princess was not the comparatively easy function that Charles' birth had been. Nor, as time went on, was this the only difference between the two children. They were, from the very start, as different from each other as chalk from cheese. Right from birth, Charles was a happy and contented child, who slept well at night and seemed to face up to life with a constant chuckle on his chubby face. Even the teething stage of infant life troubled him little. He was, in the words of one royal servant, "a perfect kid". Anne, by contrast, soon proved herself a child with a will of her own, sometimes fractious and frequently tearful.

Prince Philip was home again in the October for the christening of Anne Elizabeth Alice Louise, and was solemnly handed a bottle of orange juice and another of cod liver oil for the baby when he registered the birth. As with Charles, the christening ceremony took place at Buckingham Palace, where the godparents included Queen Elizabeth, Prince Philip's sister, Princess Margarita of Hohenlohe-Langenburg, and his uncle, Earl Mountbatten of Burma.

Between these two events, the birth of Princess Anne and her christening, Princess Elizabeth, with her husband away about his naval duties, travelled north to Scotland with her two small children for the customary royal stay at Balmoral. This, for some years to come, was to be the pattern of life for the future King . . . as it was his mother's before him, her father's before that and her father's father's before that. The pattern of the years, as the pattern of nursery days, displayed a reassuring sameness . . . weekdays in London and weekends at Windsor, Easter at Windsor summer at Balmoral, Christmas at Sandringham.

It was a pattern which was to mould and round the childhood character of the future King and, continued unbroken, rounding his character into manhood, would perhaps have ended up in producing a placid, contented, but exceedingly dull young man. His parents, however, were alive to the obvious dangers. They saw, in good time, the need to vary the traditional pattern of royal upbringing in a rapidly changing world. They realised the need to expose their son, as he grew towards manhood, to schoolday life and all the other innovations that that was to bring in its train.

IV

Despite all else she had to do as the condition of her sick father steadily worsened, despite the increasing frequency with which she was forced to leave them to carry out an ever-increasing number of royal duties, the children's mother still managed to salvage sufficient time from the royal round to play a real and active part in their upbringing. She had said once that her dearest wish was to lead a sufficiently free existence to enable her to bring up her children herself. But her father's failing health was gradually denying her that freedom and she found it difficult to gain sufficient time from the demands of royal duty to be a mother as well as a princess.

Such opportunities as she had to be with the children became doubly precious to her ... and were put to good use. She gave Charles his first simple lessons with the aid of picture books and a set of ABC building blocks. A bead-frame came in handy for teaching him to count. Between mother and son there was never any baby-talk. Trains were always trains, never 'puff-puffs'; horses were simply horses, not 'gee-gees'.

No less pleasurable to the royal mother were those nursery moments when she held her baby daughter on her knee, feeding her from a bottle, and those halcyon half-hours when she found herself free to wheel her round the garden in her carriage. Prince Philip, too, on those all-too-rare occasions when he was at home, did not consider it at all lacking in masculine dignity to be glimpsed giving Princess Anne her airing in the Clarence House garden. And for parents and children alike there was always enjoyment to be derived from the hilarious fun of the evening bath session ... wetter, soapier, and more boisterous than ever.

Prince Charles, as he grew towards boyhood, developed chubby and stubborn chinned. His hair, once it had lost the initial fairness of babyhood, proved decidedly unruly, losing its newly-induced parting and flopping back over the forehead almost as soon as it had been brushed. In looks he revealed the main characteristics of both his parents ... their blue eyes, his father's rather prominent ears, his mother's generous mouth and, when his face was in repose, her pensive brow and often serious expression. A boy with 'a gentle heart', his grandmother, the Queen, once called him, and the expression was apt. He was, even as a small child, thoughtful, serious, patient, obstinate ... and extremely dignified. Those who knew him in babyhood recall that even then there was already a regal air about him, never more apparent than in the stiffly upright manner in which he held himself during outings in his baby carriage.

His mother, when speaking of him to his nanny or to any other members of the Royal Family, referred to him as 'Charles'. He was similarly 'Charles' to everyone in the nursery, to Nanny Lightbody, 'Mamba' Anderson and the young footman whose duty it was to clean the shoes, run errands and set the table at meal-times. And 'Charles' he was to remain to the nursery staff until long after he was out of the nursery. Not until comparatively recent times, shortly after his sixteenth birthday, was it diplomatically conveyed to those who had known him from babyhood that it would be more in keeping with his status if they referred to him as 'Prince Charles' for the future.

From the outset he was always 'Prince Charles' to anyone outside the Royal Family and the nursery staff, though that was as far as the Princess went in acknowledging his special status as the future King. There was never any bowing or curtseying to him in babyhood or childhood. At least, not officially, though a former member of the royal staff insists that the previous housekeeper at Windsor Castle, a royal retainer of the old school with unchanging ideas of what was fit and proper, was seen to drop a curtsey whenever the baby Prince passed by in his pram.

Once he was out of the pram, a toy gun and a noisy tin trumpet with which he paraded the Clarence House corridors were among his favourite toys. A favourite teddy-bear became his inseparable companion. *Baba the Elephant* was a favourite story to be read aloud at bedtime, *Pop Goes the Weasel* a favourite nursery rhyme and *The Teddy Bears' Picnic* a favourite tune.

Indeed, this remained his favourite tune almost up to the time when he first went to school. A much-played recording of it accompanied him from Clarence House to Buckingham Palace after his mother became Queen, and it was a predictable choice at Windsor Castle the day the Director of Music asked him what tune he would like the band to play especially for him.

As a small child, Charles had a boy's enthusiasm for parades and uniforms and military bands. A combination of military music and marching feet could be sure to bring him rushing to the nearest window. At Windsor on one occasion, spectators listening to the music in the quadrangle suddenly came alive to the fact that the band had acquired an additional conductor in the person of the small boy who stood at the open window of the royal apartment, beating time with what appeared to be either a pencil or a short stick.

As though realising that her small son was attracting attention away from the band, his mother came into view at the window, taking his makeshift baton away from him. But the tassel of the window blind remained within his reach to serve as a replacement with which to 'conduct' the band.

Prince Charles was barely two when it was decided that he should have his portrait painted to add to his mother's personal collection of family miniatures. The honour of executing the painting was entrusted to Australian-born Stella Marks, a portrait painter well known not only in Britain and Australia, but also in the United States where she executed miniatures for many wealthy and influential families.

This was by no means her first royal miniature. She had already painted a miniature of the boy's mother, completed only three days before Charles was born, and one of his father. She arrived at Clarence House for her first sitting to find Charles and his mother both down on their hands and knees, busily building a castle of interlocking bricks on the floor. It was perhaps not what she had expected, but she promptly fell into the spirit of the occasion and knelt on the floor herself to make her preliminary sketches.

His own toys and the painter's empty tubes, which seemed to fascinate him, kept the young Prince amused and mainly still during subsequent sittings. But there was no sitting still when troops marched past Clarence House on their way to the daily changing-of-the-guard ceremony at Buckingham Palace. As soon as his ears caught the distant sound of music and the tramp of marching feet, Charles would scuttle from his chair and rush to the window, where he solemnly saluted the guards as they went past. But sometimes he saluted with the wrong hand until his mother or nanny corrected him.

Such forgivable interruptions apart, he proved himself a perfect sitter for one so young . . . patient and quiet. There was only one occasion when restlessness overcame him and he asked to get down from his chair.

"I don't think Mrs. Marks has finished yet," his nanny informed him.

He appealed to his mother, sitting at the other end of the room. But his mother was not one to interfere with nursery discipline and she, too, told him that Mrs. Marks had not yet finished.

Charles looked at the painter, an expression of wistful charm on his face, still at the midway stage between babyhood and boyhood.

"You *have* finished, haven't you, Mrs. Marks . . . *please!*"

"Of course," she said, though in fact she had not.

"I simply couldn't resist him," she explained to his mother later.

"No one ever can," said the Princess, smiling.

Young as he was, the future King, even at that tender age, already showed some awareness of his special position. Mrs. Marks was sitting one day on the nursery sofa, looking through some family photographs in company with the royal nanny.

"That's Charles," said the nanny, pointing to a particular photograph.

From behind the sofa a childish treble intervened.

"That's *Prince* Charles," her small charge corrected her.

3   *Duke of Cornwall*

I

The year of 1951 was drawing to a close. The excitement of Christmas had come and gone, all too quickly for Prince Charles and his small sister. Charles was now a sturdy little boy of three; Anne, not quite eighteen months old, was fast developing into a quicksilver sprite with bobbing blonde hair and twinkling periwinkle eyes.

They had spent Christmas as usual at Sandringham with their parents and grandparents, a festive occasion marred this year by the knowledge that parents and children were soon to be separated again. Princess Elizabeth and her husband were to leave shortly after Christmas on the first leg of the long journey to Australia and New Zealand which they were to visit on behalf of the Princess' sick father, King George VI.

But it was also, though Charles and Anne were perhaps still too young to understand, an occasion for family rejoicing because the King seemed to be making so good a recovery from long-standing ill-health and recent surgery.

The two children remained at Sandringham with their nanny while Granny and Grandpapa, as they called the King and Queen, travelled to London to bid their daughter God-speed on her departure from London airport. Then the royal grandparents returned to Sandringham to look after their grandchildren while their daughter and her husband were away about royal business.

Prince Charles was growing up to understand that these enforced separations from his parents were somehow part and parcel of the specialness of royal life. But he was still a small boy as well as a Prince and childish understanding could not always prevent him from shedding a few tears when the time came to say goodbye. A packet of chocolate cigarettes as a parting gift from Mummy

31

had helped to console him the previous autumn when he said goodbye to them at Clarence House as they left on their longest trip so far, a lengthy tour of Canada, from Montreal, Ottawa and Toronto to Calgary and Vancouver and back again, with a two-day side-trip to Washington. As always when she was away, Princess Elizabeth telephoned Clarence House frequently for news of how the children were coming along and for Charles, now of an age when he knew all about telephones, there was the excitement of being able to talk to Mummy all those thousands of miles away.

Charles was taken to meet his parents when they got back from that long, long trip. It was three days after his third birthday and everyone who glimpsed him commented upon his likeness to his father . . . the same trick of stuffing his hands deep in his pockets, the same habit of walking around with his hands clasped behind his back.

He revealed, too, that he had inherited his father's thrusting, inquiring, inquisitive nature to a considerable degree. He was always asking questions, wanting to know how this worked and why something else was the way it was. In particular, his father's naval uniform exercised a fascination for him and there was one occasion when he asked so many questions, with his father spending so long explaining the significance and purpose of his various badges and decorations, that Prince Philip was almost late for an engagement he was attending.

Not naturally the most patient of men, Prince Philip was not always quite so tolerant of the boy's frequent questions.

"Don't ask so many questions, Charles," he reproved his son on one occasion when the boy's questioning interrupted his father's conversation with someone else.

But, on balance, Prince Philip was a thoughtful and considerate father, always willing to find time for the children, joining in their games, reading them stories at bedtime. He had that happy knack, given to few adults, of being able to get down to the trusting, wide-eyed level of childhood without any appearance of condescension.

The excitement of that homecoming from Canada was further

enlivened by the gifts the royal parents brought back for the children . . . cowboy outfits and colourful Indian headdresses which they were not yet big enough to wear, but would soon grow into; polar-bear rugs to go beside their beds.

And now, at Sandringham, there was some small degree of consolation for Charles in wondering what gifts Mummy and Papa would bring back this time. Princess Elizabeth, as she was leaving, had promised "some lovely presents" for the two children if they were good during the long six months she expected to be away.

But something was to happen which drove all thoughts of presents from everyone's minds and considerably shortened the anticipated six months of separation.

II

Granny—Queen Elizabeth—was a frequent visitor to the children's nursery during that Christmas stay at Sandringham, joining them in the games of childhood, teaching Charles how to play ludo and snakes and ladders, explaining the story of the Nativity with the aid of a cut-out model which was a nursery adornment. But Grandpapa—the King—never visited the nursery. Recovering in health though he seemed to be, it was as though he found the company of small children too much for him, and the only occasions on which he saw Charles and Anne were when they went along to join him and Granny at tea-time.

Then, on February 5, this normal pattern of life was broken in a rather strange way. The King had recovered sufficiently to go shooting. He was seemingly on top of his form, laughing and chatting animatedly, and there might have been nothing wrong with him. He returned from the shooting field, removed his boots and went along to rest in the ground-floor bedroom which had been specially prepared to save him the additional exertion of going up and down stairs. His tea was taken in to him on a tray.

The Queen and Princess Margaret were still out, having driven across Norfolk to visit a friend, artist Edward Seago, in his studio home. They were still away when the King, his rest over, came out of his room again, walked to the elevator and rode up to the first floor.

Charles and Anne were having supper in the nursery when the King walked in and they greeted him eagerly after their childish fashion. The nursery staff were, of course, surprised and delighted to see him. It was his first visit to the nursery during the whole of that stay at Sandringham ... and no one could foresee that it would also be his last.

He sat with the children while they had supper, talking to them of this and that, answering their childish questions. Then, at bedtime, he went into each of the bedrooms in turn, tucking them in and saying a quiet prayer with them before finally saying goodnight.

Then he went downstairs again to have dinner with his wife and younger daughter, strolled briefly in the grounds, listened to the latest radio bulletin about Princess Elizabeth's tour and went to bed with a magazine in his hand.

Some time that night he died quietly in his sleep.

III

The two children were having breakfast the following morning when word first reached the staff of the royal nursery that the King was dead. From an early hour there had been sad and dramatic comings and goings, though none of this trickled through to the nursery on the first floor. The King's valet having failed to rouse his master when he ran his daily bath at half-past seven, an urgent telephone call had summoned Dr. J. L. B. Ansell, Surgeon Apothecary to the Royal Household at Sandringham, from his farmhouse home at neighbouring Wolferton. But there was, sadly, nothing he could do when he got there.

The King was dead. His twenty-five-year-old daughter, four thousand miles away in Kenya, was now Her Most Excellent Majesty Queen Elizabeth II, even though she did not yet know it. And the small, serious-faced boy of three quietly eating his breakfast in the first-floor nursery was now the Duke of Cornwall in accordance with a royal charter dating back to Edward II in 1337, and destined to be the Prince of Wales and the future King.

But the important thing that grey, tragic February morning was that the lives of the royal children, Charles and Anne, should go on much as usual, as far as possible untouched by the sad and unexpected death of the Grandpapa to whom they were so attached.

"Their lives must not be affected by what has happened," said their Granny, the Queen Mother as she now was.

Except for their meals, the two children spent most of that day, from breakfast to bedtime, out of doors in the spacious grounds of Sandringham House, where the tenseness and grief inside the house could not reach them, and where their eager cries and bright laughter could not be heard by those who mourned the King's passing.

At half-past four that afternoon, when they returned to the house, instead of going along to have tea with Granny as usual, they were taken straight up to the nursery. Prince Charles, in particular, seemed puzzled and perhaps a little disturbed by this departure from the normal routine. It was time his Grandpapa's death was explained to him.

But the Queen Mother, cloaked in her own grief, could not bear to break the sad news to the children, and it was left to the royal nanny, Helen Lightbody, to explain to Charles what had happened. Of course, at three, he did not fully understand and it was left that Grandpapa had 'gone away'.

At bedtime that evening the Queen Mother paid her customary goodnight visit to the nursery. She was in mourning and her face was pale and drawn. Perhaps Charles wondered why she looked so sad; perhaps his young mind linked her sadness with news of Grandpapa's going away.

If it did, such thoughts were driven speedily from his mind by the news that Mummy was coming home the following day. For him and Anne, it was wonderful, happy, exciting news.

IV

Easter, in accordance with royal tradition, was spent at Windsor Castle, and the Queen, as she now was, made convenient use of the fact to move from Clarence House to the vaster, more impersonal atmosphere of Buckingham Palace. Anxious to upset the children's normal life as little as possible, she had their new nursery at Buckingham Palace laid out as nearly as possible identical with the old nursery at Clarence House ... the same chintz curtains at the windows, the same winged armchairs, the same glass-fronted cabinet to hold toys and books, even the same stout fireguard.

As far as the new young Duke of Cornwall was concerned, there was little need for his mother to fear that he would become unsettled by the uprooting from Clarence House and the transplanting at Buckingham Palace. On the contrary, he appeared considerably intrigued by the vast palace, with its scores of rooms and its labyrinth of long, red-carpeted corridors, which was now his home. Like his father, he was soon busy exploring.

Prince Philip is reputed to have poked his inquiring features into every one of the 600-plus rooms which constitute Buckingham Palace. The story is perhaps slightly exaggerated, but it is a fact that he penetrated as deep as the fuel stores in the basement and as high as the servants' living quarters on the topmost floor during those early days when his wife first became Queen.

Prince Charles had no opportunity to explore quite so widely, but he was soon trotting everywhere about the nursery floor and in the vicinity of his parents' apartment on the floor below—he always seemed to trot; never walked—with the royal corgis, Susan and Sugar, frisking at his heels, and, later, with a diminutive figure adorned by a bobbing blonde topknot hurrying after him with eager cries of, "Wait for me, Charles ... please wait for me".

There was one occasion when he somehow eluded the usual watchful eyes of the royal nannies and set out along the wide, red-carpeted corridor of the nursery suite. A member of the Queen's staff encountered him, some time later and a floor lower down, still heading purposefully away from the direction of the nursery.

Asked where he was going, the young Prince vouchsafed the information that he was 'exploring'.

He showed much the same inquisitiveness concerning his new surroundings during the royal weekends at Windsor Castle. His nanny, who slept in the same room, was perhaps under the impression that he was playing with his toys in the day nursery on those mornings when he clambered out of bed half-an-hour earlier than usual. In fact, on such occasions, he was usually 'exploring'. One morning, quite early, he surprised one of the servants making morning tea for others of the staff. Boy-like, he begged to be allowed to help.

As a result, another member of the staff, still in bed, answered a tap at his bedroom door to find the small future King standing there, teacup in hand. "I've brought you your tea," said Prince Charles.

For a time after that, during weekends at Windsor, it became something of a habit for the small Prince to help with the morning tea. Then the practice stopped. Perhaps Prince Charles tired of the game; perhaps his nanny came to hear of it and disapproved.

The many strange, new faces of royal officials and servants he so constantly encountered during those early days at Buckingham Palace bothered him not at all.

"Hello," he would say. "I'm Charles. Who are you, please?"

Soon he was greeting them with a brisk, "Good morning," and extending a small, royal hand.

Wisely, his parents tried to cushion him as much as possible from the significance of his new and important position as the next monarch. But there were, even if the future King was too young to appreciate the fact, some significant changes taking place in his own life and the lives of those around him. Like any other young woman, Princess Elizabeth, as she was at the time, had taken her husband's name of Mountbatten upon marriage. But two months after she succeeded to the Throne, the Queen, as she now was, acting, so it is said, upon the advice of the late Sir Winston Churchill, reverted to the family name of Windsor, and the royal edict which gave effect to the change applied also to the small, bright, tousled-haired, inquisitive three-year-old who was heir to the Throne. Of less historic but more practical moment perhaps, was her appointment of a royal physician-paediatrician in the person of Mr. (later Sir) Wilfrid Sheldon to watch over the health of her children—the first such appointment in royal history.

To Charles and Anne, their new nursery on the third floor of Buckingham Palace was like a little self-contained world of its own. Cornerstone of nursery life was the day nursery, a large, airy, high-ceilinged room with walls of duck-egg blue on the very corner of the palace, looking out to the front along the Mall and overlooking Constitution Hill at the side. Several oil paintings hung on the walls . . . a naval scene, a view of Newhaven Harbour, a Tasmanian landscape and the symbolically-entitled *Drake's Drum*. Later, after the Coronation, these were joined by a painting of the coronation procession passing through Admiralty Arch on its way back to Buckingham Palace.

On the marble fireplace stood photographs of the children's parents and one of their great-grandmother, Queen Mary. A cuckoo clock signalled the passing hours. A glass-fronted cabinet held a collection of glass and china knick-knacks—horses, mice and other diminutive animals—and silver miniatures, including a miniature coffee set which had once belonged to the Queen and Princess Margaret, as well as a number of beautifully-fashioned model ships securely imprisoned in their bottles. The cupboards below held the children's books and games and toys.

Communicating doors linked the day nursery with the children's bedrooms, each with their polar-bear rugs, their bedside lamps— Anne's resembling a duck and Charles' a rabbit—and their identical prints of the *Madonna and Child*. Both rooms were furnished simply enough with white-painted dressing tables and built-in wardrobes. But a single glance was sufficient to tell which room was Anne's and which her brother's. Anne's room, inevitably, had two or three dolls scattered about it. In Charles' room, dolls were replaced by miniature cars while a toy fort with its guardian soldiers stood in one corner.

Neither of the children slept alone. At night, Nanny Lightbody occupied the same room as Prince Charles while Mabel Anderson provided company for his small sister. A further precaution was the microphone fixed to the wall beside each bed. Linked to a speaker in the day nursery, it gave prompt warning if either of the children was restless or fretful following bedtime.

On the landing outside the nursery, a glass-fronted cabinet held more dolls. But these were dolls with which Anne never played, a collection of official gifts which was to grow and grow as her parents' travels extended to all parts of the world. A similar cabinet in the Centre Room overlooking the palace balcony held a matching collection of model boats given to Prince Charles.

The Queen, conscious of the dangers inherent for those born to high station, was insistent that her two small children must not be spoiled or treated so that they came to regard themselves as very special little people. Newspapers containing photographs of the children were carefully hidden away where small eyes could not see them. Food fads were seldom tolerated at meal-times. The children were not permitted to help themselves to chocolates or candy. They had to ask . . . and never until after lunch.

Childish misbehaviour was suitably punished as in less regal homes. There were seldom spankings, though Prince Philip reportedly spanked Charles on one occasion for pulling a face at a crowd of people. There was equally an occasion later when he spanked Anne for a display of tantrums over what she was to wear. But the more customary nursery punishment for childish misdemeanours was a short period spent alone in the bedroom or nursery bathroom without toys, books or other childhood diversions to help pass the time.

Politeness was a 'must' at all times . . . a lesson their mother, the Queen, had had drilled into her during her own childhood days. There was one occasion, during the Queen's childhood, when she addressed the man who wound the royal clocks by his surname, omitting the small courtesy of adding any prefix. Her mother chanced to overhear and called her to one side.

A moment or two later the small Princess went back to the clock-winder. "I'm sorry I didn't 'mister' you," she apologised.

Charles, at this early stage of his life, was similarly reared in the tradition of good manners. He was taught to say 'Please' if he wanted anything, and 'Thank you' when he got it. He absorbed the lesson readily enough, and equally readily, passed it on to Anne. On one occasion, at the end of a railway journey, he took her firmly by the hand and led her along the railway platform towards the front of the train.

"Come along, Anne," he said in big-brotherly fashion. "We have to say 'Thank you' to the engine driver."

Just as his mother, at an early age, had helped to develop a sense of social responsibility in the irrepressible Princess Margaret—and occasionally reprimanded her for an untoward display of high spirits—so Charles now took a similar hand in the training of his small sister.

"This is my sister, Anne," he would announce by way of introduction, occasionally throwing in an item of additional interest about her. "When she grows up, Anne is going to have her ears dugged out for ear-rings like Mummy and Margo," he informed one visitor to the royal nursery.

"Now say 'how do you do', Anne," the young Prince would instruct his still younger sister. Or, "Now say 'thank you', Anne" when she had been given something or helped in some way. And, on one occasion after she had fallen down and he had rushed to her rescue, "I'm always having trouble with you".

Anne, at this stage of her life and for some years to come, hero-worshipped her 'big' brother. Everything he did, she had to do, too. If he played at soldiers with his toy gun and trumpet, she would forsake her dolls to join in. If he up-ended his tricycle to 'repair' it, she would similarly set to work on hers. When he rushed to the window to salute as the guards marched past, she would copy him.

"Girls don't salute," Charles informed her firmly on one occasion.

From an early age, both children were trained to do things for themselves. If either of them wanted perhaps a clean handkerchief, they were told where it was and sent to fetch it. Prince Philip, in particular, was insistent that they must not be brought up expecting to be waited upon at every turn, as he plainly showed on one occasion when Charles came into the room leaving the door open behind him.

One of the servants hurried to close it.

"Leave it alone, man," Prince Philip ordered, briskly. "He's got hands. Let him do it himself."

And the young Prince was sent back to close the door behind him.

The Queen, despite all else she had to do in her new role as monarch, made time whenever she could to be with her children. She had inherited from her mother the sound axiom that a happy and secure family life in childhood is the basis for all that comes later. This she put into practice.

New to the throne, initially she drew a firm line between monarchy and motherhood. Neither Charles nor Anne was permitted to go to her sitting room, which served also as her study, during what their mother came to regard as her 'working hours'. Later, however, as she came more and more to take the arduous role of monarchy in her swinging stride, she was able to relax this rule for Andrew and Edward.

But even at the outset of monarchy, what free time she could command was devoted to the children. Every morning, immediately after breakfast, they came down to see her. They had been brought up from almost as soon as they could walk to bow and curtsey to their grandparents, the King and Queen, and to their great-grandmother, Queen Mary. Now that their mother was Queen they accorded her the same dignity, pausing in the doorway for Charles to give a deferential bow and Anne to drop a diminutive curtsey.

The Queen gave instructions to the nursery staff that such formality was to cease immediately. From then on, the children, whenever they came to see her, ran straight towards her to greet her and Papa with spanking kisses.

Lunchtime would often find the Queen vanishing upstairs in the direction of the nursery. At half-past five the children came downstairs again and from then until bedtime their mother's time was exclusively theirs. Even the Prime Minister's regular Tuesday evening call at the palace to discuss affairs of state with the new monarch was not permitted to interfere with this evening play-time. At the Queen's request, he postponed it until after the children's bedtime.

On fine afternoons in summer, mother and children would go out into the palace gardens, where the two children played in the sandpit or exercised on a climbing frame while mother watched. A knotted rope slung from the branch of a tree provided another test for young limbs. Sometimes they would have Harvey out on the lawn to play with. Harvey was Prince Charles' pet rabbit, a white Angora, which he had brought with him from Clarence House and which now occupied a hutch and run near the garden entrance of the palace.

On these afternoons, tea took the form of a picnic in the summerhouse. On other afternoons, toys were brought out on the carpet of the Queen's sitting room, a play session interspersed, for Charles at least, with further lessons in reading, writing and counting from his mother. Or mother and children would sit watching the children's programmes on television together.

If Prince Philip was home, this tea-time playtime would often become considerably more boisterous. Out they would all go into the broad corridor flanking the royal apartment, father, mother, children and dogs, for a family game of football, with the corgis scampering and yelping after the ball, while the marble busts which line the corridor looked on unblinkingly. And afterwards, hot and thirsty from their exertions, the children would rush to Papa's study to refresh themselves with soft drinks from the refrigerator he had had newly installed.

For Prince Charles, the vast rooms and long corridors of Buckingham Palace offered opportunities for endless fresh diversions . . . wide, open spaces along which to bounce balls for the corgis to pursue, a proving ground for a new, pedal-operated horse and cart (though he could not always avoid an occasional collision with the antique furnishings). The Grand Hall downstairs became a racetrack for a scaled-down car, coloured British racing green, a magnificent toy with imitation gears, brakes, lights, indicators, horn, wing mirrors and even a musical box radio. The car was garaged behind one of the marble statues which adorn the Grand Hall, with royal pages and footmen persuaded to act as track officials or policemen, according to the game being played, by the small royal driver-owner.

The heated indoor swimming pool at the rear of the palace provided another outlet for boyish energy. At half-past five in the afternoon the small sturdy figure of the future King, a bathrobe concealing his diminutive swimming trunks, would appear in the corridor which led to his father's study.

"Where's Papa?" he wanted to know.

He was ready for his daily swimming lesson and off they would go together, the tall, athletic father and his small, sturdy son, in the direction of the pool. If Prince Philip was not free on a particular day, his private secretary, Michael Parker, would deputise for him in giving the boy a swimming lesson.

The story that Charles was afraid of the water has no foundation in fact. He was, admittedly, more nervous than Anne where horses were concerned. But in the water he was completely at ease, and even before he started lessons in the nursery schoolroom he could already swim the length of the palace pool.

At bedtime, or a little before, the Queen would take the children back upstairs to the nursery. Mother and children rode up in the lift while Papa bounded long-legged up the stairs, the corgis yapping at his heels, in a race to see who would be first to the nursery door. Bedtime was invariably the occasion for hilarious bathroom splashing and bedroom pillow-fighting. Laughter and shouting echoed from the nursery suite, a combination of noise which royal servants insisted, doubtless with some slight exaggeration, could be heard 'all over the palace'.

Exaggeration or not, it was as though, with the advent of Prince Charles and his live-wire little sister, the vast, echoing rooms and long, sombre corridors of the palace came suddenly to life.

4   *Journey to Tobruk*

Gradually and almost imperceptibly, the future King absorbed a consciousness of who he was, and some understanding of the high and special position he would one day occupy. He mastered the lessons of royal behaviour in such matters as politeness and punctuality. He had, from birth, become accustomed to sentries presenting arms, policemen saluting and onlookers applauding as he came and went. He absorbed rather than learned the lessons of regal dignity. He understood, for instance, that it was not done for a Prince, even one of four years old, to munch candy in public. There was one reported occasion when he went out with his Granny, the Queen Mother. He was noticeably sucking candy as the royal car reached its destination, with the usual crowd of onlookers waiting to witness its arrival. Then, as he clambered from the car, at least one eagle-eyed spectator saw him take it from his mouth and pass it to the gloved hand of the Queen Mother.

The approaching ceremony of Coronation intrigued him immensely. One day, in his travels about the palace, he chanced upon some royal servants engaged in the painstaking and delicate task of brushing the long, weighty robe of royal purple which the Queen would wear for part of the Coronation ceremony. It was perhaps something more than mere childlike curiosity which prompted the young Prince to ask what they were doing. It was explained to him that they were preparing 'the Queen's robe'.

The information seemed to puzzle him. He knew already, as we have told, that he was 'Prince Charles', but perhaps did not yet fully understand what the title signified. After all, he was only four years old. Certainly, from the question which followed, it would seem clear that he did not yet understand the full significance of the high position held by the young woman he knew as 'Mummy'.

"Who is the Queen?" he wanted to know.

"Why, your Mummy, of course."

It was in such chance fashion rather than from any system of formal instruction that the young Prince acquired his first simple understanding of monarchy. The approaching Coronation provided other similar lessons. From the royal nursery he could see some of the wooden stands being erected to accommodate those who would watch the Coronation procession. Martial music and marching feet still captivated him and he was constantly at the nursery windows watching the troops rehearse their part in all this colourful pageantry. On Coronation morning he was awakened early by the blare of trumpets, the rub-a-dub of drums and the clatter of horses' hooves. While his small sister, Princess Anne, had to remain content with a view from the nursery window of their mother's departure for Westminster Abbey in the great gold coach with its painted roof, Charles was excited by the know-ledge that he would be going to the Abbey itself.

Nanny Lightbody spruced him up for the occasion in a frilled shirt and short trousers of white silk, slicking his unruly hair into place more firmly than usual in the hope that, for once, it would remain in position, and drove with him to the Abbey, where they entered by a private door at the rear. Unobtrusively he was escorted to the front row of the royal box where he slipped into a seat between his Granny and 'Margo', as he always called Princess Margaret. A footstool to stand on lent him additional height, enabling him to see more clearly all that was going on.

He reached his place just as that part of the ceremony known as the Anointing was about to begin. The crimson robe in which the Queen had arrived at the Abbey had been removed. A cloth-of-gold canopy was in the act of being raised above her head to screen her partially from view as hands, head and breast were anointed with holy oil. But silent and unobtrusive though Charles' arrival had been, his mother had noticed. She glanced his way and for a fleeting moment a half-smile of reassurance lit up her features, the only time she permitted herself to look other than completely serious during all that long ceremony.

As he stood on his footstool, hands and chin resting on the balustrade of the royal box, Charles, from force of habit, smoothed his hair with his hand. He put his hand to his nose and apparently liked the scent of the dressing which had been employed to keep his hair in place, for he extended his hand towards the Queen Mother so that she could smell it for herself.

"Smell, Granny," he is supposed to have said. "Doesn't it smell nice?"

So engrossed was he by all that was going on, so still and well behaved in his concentration, that he was permitted to stay at the Abbey longer than had been originally planned, with Granny explaining in simple terms all that was happening and answering his many whispered questions.

Granny's Coronation lesson seems to have made a considerable impression on his young mind. A visitor to the palace some time afterwards recalls Charles and Anne at a window overlooking the forecourt where the Guards were carrying out their intricate and traditional drill movements. "We're watching the Coronation," Anne explained.

At her age, the mistake was understandable. But Charles, some twenty-one months older, knew better and was quick to correct his small sister. It wasn't the Coronation, he said; it was the changing of the guard. And he was perhaps repeating something the Queen Mother had told him during that visit to Westminster Abbey when he added that there wouldn't be another Coronation for a long time "and that will be mine".

If it sounds a perhaps somewhat improbable conversation between two such young children, we can only add that we are assured that it took place. And it should be remembered that to the two royal children in their palace home, such things as the changing of the guard were, even then, familiar and almost commonplace occurrences.

Indeed, the pageantry and ceremony which they witnessed as part of the process of growing up became absorbed into their nursery games. At Sandringham at Christmas the young Prince's

47

gifts included a toy sword and a swashbuckling cloak of red velvet. For most youngsters, swords are symbols of fighting and Charles, too, waged his make-believe battles with imaginary foes. But royal environment had also taught him another use for a sword which would surely not have occurred to any ordinary youngster.

He was running along one of the corridors at Sandringham, sword in hand, the cloak about his shoulders, when he encountered two of the royal menservants with whom he was especially friendly. It apparently entered his young mind that now was the opportunity to reward their friendship in suitable fashion. He asked them to kneel down. They did so, entering into the spirit of the game. What followed showed that the future King, even at that age, had knowledge of royal investitures.

In turn, he tapped each of them lightly on both shoulders with his toy sword, saying "Arise, Sir——"

'Coronations' was another favourite game at this time, with Charles wearing his Christmas cloak. Anne had no cloak, but she made up for the deficiency by borrowing a tablecloth which she draped around her shoulders so that it trailed along the floor behind her. Dressed in this fashion, the two children would solemnly parade up and down the red carpet of the nursery corridor.

"I'm the King," Charles explained to someone who surprised them at this game, "and Anne is the Queen."

II

A few days after his fifth birthday, Prince Charles, his small sister beside him, stood on a stool at one of the palace windows to wave goodbye to Mummy and Papa as they drove off to London Airport on the first stage of the long journey which was to take them 50,000 miles to ten different countries over the course of the next six months.

Children and parents alike were doubtless saddened at the prospect of yet another separation . . . and a long one. But the Queen was not worried at the thought of leaving her children. Parting from them was something to which she had become accustomed in recent years. Besides, she knew she was leaving them in good hands. She had complete confidence in the staff of the royal nursery, and there was always the children's beloved 'Granny'—the Queen Mother—to keep an additional eye on things while she was away.

But while she may not have worried about them, she certainly missed them, as they missed her. In Kingston, Jamaica, on the first night of that long separation, she slept with photographs of the two children beside her on the bedside table. Later, in Australia, she made the frank and mother-like admission, "I'm really looking forward to seeing them again".

To keep Charles occupied while she was away, and thus lessen the pangs of separation for him as well as maintain the continuity of the lessons she had been giving him herself since babyhood, the Queen engaged a governess and arranged for regular morning lessons in one of the rooms forming part of the nursery suite. For the position of governess, her choice fell upon Miss Katherine Peebles, a tall, dark, Glasgow-born Scot with previous experience as governess to the children of Princess Marina, who was then the Duchess of Kent. Firm and skilful in her handling of children, Miss Peebles was perhaps selected by the Queen, in part at least, because of her recognised ability to bring out the latent character in a child. As much as anything, the Queen may have hoped that she would find ways and means of counteracting the shyness which is a family trait of the Windsors and which Prince Charles, during those early, formative years, showed some sign of having inherited.

By the time he was first introduced to Miss Peebles—or 'Mispy' (Miss P.) as he and Anne came to call her—the young Prince, thanks to his mother's tuition, could already tell the time and write his official signature, 'Charles', in bold, if somewhat shaky, capital letters. He had already begun to have dancing lessons, designed as much as anything to give him poise and confidence.

Every morning after breakfast, while his mother was away on her long tour of the Commonwealth, Prince Charles went along for lessons with Miss Peebles in her sitting room which also doubled as the nursery schoolroom. A blackboard and easel were erected each day when lessons commenced and removed when they were

49

over. He sat not in a schoolroom desk, but at a table. The Queen had perhaps not forgotten her own difficulty in childhood when she had to sit sideways at a desk for which she had grown too big.

Miss Peebles taught him scripture and history, drawing and painting, reading, writing and simple arithmetic. French was not introduced into the curriculum until some little time later. A large globe of the world, on which the young Prince could follow his parents' travels, added to the fun of geography lessons.

Schoolroom discipline for this one small, solitary pupil was kind, yet firm. "Children have to be made to realise that they cannot always have their own way," Miss Peebles had said on one occasion, and this principle she now applied to the future King just as she would have done to any other child. She encouraged the boy where she thought he was capable of more, but did not press him unduly in subjects with which he was not yet at ease, following the maxim that each child is first and foremost an individual with particular talents and certain weaknesses.

The two children, Charles and Anne, spent part of the long six months while their parents were away with 'Granny'. At weekends they went with her to Royal Lodge at Windsor, where one of their favourite playthings was the little cottage with the thatched roof which the people of Wales had given to their mother, the Queen, when she was a girl of six. Too large for any playroom, the cottage, with its electric light and running water, its diminutive bathroom, stands in the grounds of Royal Lodge, and Charles and Anne were delighted to discover, as their mother had discovered before them, that even Grannies could get inside by bobbing their heads to negotiate the tiny doorway.

The Queen Mother is an enthusiastic gardener, never happier than when pottering about the gardens in old clothes and a floppy felt hat. Charles, of course, wanted to help her. He had a toy wheelbarrow and now Granny unearthed for him a miniature set of gardening tools which his mother and Princess Margaret had had as children. Enthusiastically, he set to work 'helping Granny'. The Queen Mother continued with her gardening chores, leaving him to amuse himself, and it was not until some time later that she discovered him patiently and carefully digging up a whole row of newly-planted bulbs!

At Christmas, with their parents still away, Charles and Anne went with Granny to Sandringham. Charles had always been musically inclined and at Sandringham that year, when the local carol-singers called as they made their Christmas rounds, his hands strayed continually towards a fiddle one of the carollers had been using and which was now resting on a nearby chair.

The Queen Mother noticed what he was doing. "Now leave that alone, Charles. You might break it," she cautioned him. But before the carol-singers left again she asked if her small grandson might try the fiddle and helped him hold it under his chin while he drew the bow tentatively across the strings.

Though his parents were away, for Charles that Christmas of 1953 was still an enjoyable and exciting one. There was all the fun of unwrapping the gifts Mummy and Papa had left already packed before setting off on their long trip around the world, among them the home-made Christmas stockings which the Queen herself had filled with an exciting selection of candy and small toys.

Then, on Christmas morning, there was *the* telephone call . . . with Charles and Anne standing either side of the Queen Mother, eagerly awaiting their turn to wish Mummy and Papa a happy Christmas all those thousands of miles away in New Zealand.

III

There was an even more exciting adventure to come . . . a long voyage aboard the new royal yacht *Britannia*, all the way out to Tobruk to meet Mummy and Papa at the end of their long round-the-world tour.

For weeks beforehand, the coming trip was almost the only subject of conversation in the royal nursery. Both children could talk of little else. As the time of departure drew near they helped to do their own packing in two large brown leather trunks with brass labels, one inscribed 'Prince Charles' and the other 'Princess Anne'.

'Granny' and 'Margo'—the Queen Mother and Princess

Margaret—accompanied them to Portsmouth to see them set sail. Nanny Lightbody, Charles' governess, Miss Peebles, and the under-nanny, Mabel Anderson, went aboard *Britannia* with them to accompany them on the voyage. So did a miscellaneous collection of toys designed to help time pass if the two children became bored and to divert their attention in the event of feeling seasick ... Charles' teddy bear, tricycle and pedal car, Anne's tricycle, dolls' house and some favourite dolls.

But there was no question of either Charles or Anne becoming bored or seasick. There was too much to do, too much to see. From the moment they went aboard, with Charles striding purposefully along the respectful line of attendant sailors while Anne danced and bobbed along behind, murmuring a quiet "How do you do?" to each sailor as she passed, until they were reunited with Mummy and Papa in Tobruk there was never a dull moment. Initially, as the two youngsters found their sea-legs, they were perhaps slightly under the weather, not eating as heartily as usual. But neither of them was actually seasick.

For Charles, even if he was too young to appreciate the fact, the voyage also offered a welcome respite from the petticoat government of the royal nursery, his days at sea rendered the more exciting because they were spent not in the company of his nanny and governess, but with two sturdy young seamen, members of *Britannia's* crew specially selected to keep a weather eye on him and his young sister.

With his newfound friends as expert guides, Prince Charles explored the vessel almost from stem to stern. He visited the engine room and was frequently to be found on the bridge, where a new game of make-believe took the form of pretending he was steering the ship. For journeys around the deck, his pedal car and tricycle, time-tested favourites, were obliged to surrender pride of place to a new form of royal transport in the shape of a gaily-painted toy boat mounted on wheels. He took photographs of passing ships with a box camera, built castles in the sand-box on the sun-deck, paddled in the inflatable pool. Perhaps more enjoyable than anything else was the thrill of splashing barefooted with bucket and mop as he and Anne helped the crew to swab the deck.

At Tobruk, while the Queen and Prince Philip were still ashore, being hosted by King Idris of Libya, the royal children remained aboard the yacht, eagerly awaiting the long-anticipated reunion with their parents. It is one of the penalties of royal birth that personal life must so often take second place to public occasion, and when the Queen reached the yacht there was still the small ceremony of being piped aboard to be enacted with members of her entourage around her, the crew drawn up to attention and the ship's officers waiting to greet her. Only when this was over was she free at last to turn her attention to the waiting children. Charles, at five, was perhaps not yet of an age to differentiate between the official and the unofficial, often so interwoven for royalty as to be almost indistinguishable. Everyone else had shaken hands with Mummy and now he, too, held out a small polite hand.

"Not you, darling," the Queen was heard to say before the drawing room door closed upon the privacy of her reunion with her children.

For the two children, the voyage home was hardly less exciting than the trip out, though the weather, for a time, turned cold and rough. It was the Queen's first trip aboard the new royal yacht and initially the rather pronounced rolling motion of the vessel (later reduced by the fitting of stabilisers) was inclined to upset her. But Charles and Anne had no such qualms. Their young sea-legs were by now well accustomed to *Britannia's* rolling.

They went ashore at Malta and again at Gibraltar, where they were taken to see the Rock's famous Barbary apes. Anne, not yet four, found the antics of the apes highly diverting, even when one used her shoulder as a springboard to gain access to a higher perch. But Charles, nearly two years older and more cautious in character, was concerned for the safety of Nanny Lightbody when one of the apes took a flying leap on to her back.

At Gibraltar there were more gifts for the children to be added to all those their parents had brought back for them from their long, long tour. For Anne, there was a magnificent dolls' house, some ten feet long and four feet wide, with taps and lights that really worked, a working fountain in the garden, and furnished down to the smallest detail, even to books in the book-cases and tiny sheets and blankets on the beds. For Charles there was a real boy's toy, a large-scale model of the Rock of Gibraltar, with a working model railway, just like the real thing, running right through it.

Back in England, this model of Gibraltar was taken to Windsor and set up initially in a room adjoining Prince Philip's sitting room. Later it was moved to a basement air raid shelter which Prince Philip had converted into a playroom for the youngsters—and, incidentally, for himself! He and Charles, with Anne clamouring to join in, adjourned there frequently to play with the model and, later, with a model of the Paris Metro which the Queen was given for Charles during her state visit to France.

"That will amuse his father," she said as she accepted this French gift for her small son, showing that she knew a thing or two about fathers as well as about children.

5   *A Royal Revolution*

I

Prince Charles was six. But he was not, whatever his parents may have thought to the contrary, any ordinary six-year-old. In a country where formal education, for most youngsters, starts at five, he had not yet been to school. There was a whole range of ordinary, everyday pursuits, familiar to other children, which was quite foreign to him. Set against that, he had his own range of experience which, in certain directions at least, extended far beyond that of the normal six-year-old.

He had already journeyed as far east as Tobruk. He had seen his mother being crowned as Queen, and the apes being fed on the Rock of Gibraltar. In June, 1955, he experienced his first flight, returning from Aberdeen to London.

But while it was his first flight, it was not the first time he had been in an aircraft. The previous March his Granny, the Queen Mother, had taken him to London Airport to greet Princess Margaret on her return from the West Indies.

"Please, may I see where the pilot sits?" Charles had asked.

He was taken along to the flight cabin and not only shown the pilot's seat, but allowed to sit in it.

"Do I really look like a pilot, Granny?" he wanted to know.

The Queen Mother assured him that he did, but added that he would perhaps look even more like one when he was somewhat bigger.

Now, in the course of his first flight, he again asked if he could go through to the pilot's cabin and spent twenty fascinating boyhood minutes sitting in the co-pilot's seat alongside the aircraft's skipper.

Princess Anne made the flight with him, but far less happily. She was, at this time, suffering from a childhood ear infection which the air trip did nothing to help, and she was looking unusually pale and rather unwell when the aircraft finally touched down at London.

For Prince Charles, lessons in the nursery schoolroom at Buckingham Palace were proceeding well. By now, French—which his mother can speak fluently—had been added to the original curriculum and three times each week the young Prince made his way to what became known as the 'Centre Schoolroom', overlooking the famous Buckingham Palace balcony, for lessons with a tutor from the Lycées Français. He was, additionally, learning the piano under the tuition of concert pianist Hilda Bor and could already give passable renditions of several familiar Scottish airs on the Steinway grand on which he practised. Dancing lessons, in company with Princess Anne and a number of small friends, continued on Wednesday afternoons when Madame Vacani, who had taught the Queen and Princess Margaret to dance, and her niece, Betty, visited the palace for this purpose. Anne and her young friends were learning the rudiments of ballet. When this was over, Charles and a number of other small boys would join the class to partner the girls in a short session of Scottish and ballroom dancing.

But all work and no play would have made Charles, like Jack, a dull boy. So there was always plenty of play, plenty of fresh air and outdoor exercise, plenty of fun. There was, in addition to the normal birthday and Christmas parties, for one of which the Queen thoughtfully imported a children's slide which the youngsters enjoyed far more than ordinary party games, a special party for a few selected friends on Guy Fawkes Day. After dark, the youngsters went out into the palace gardens where the gardeners had built a giant bonfire of old wood and dead branches. Perched on top of the bonfire—so high up that a ladder had had to be used to get it into place—was a guy which Charles and Anne had helped to make, stuffing it with straw, fitting it out with a pair of trousers one of the royal footmen had discarded and an old felt hat, with the lifelike effect enhanced by a paper mask covering the face.

The bonfire was set alight and the fireworks were let off, Prince

Philip taking charge of the 'bangers' while the Queen carefully supervised the bonfire with the aid of a garden rake. Prince Charles and the other youngsters were permitted to hold sparklers and similar 'safe' fireworks in their hands, though the Queen always ensured that they were wearing gloves on such occasions to safeguard against possible mishaps.

Like many other small children, Charles and Anne, at this stage of their lives, were addicted to 'dressing up' games. A large chest which stood in the corridor flanking the royal nursery became their passport to a magic world of make-believe. Gradually, over the years of childhood, it became crammed with almost everything the heart of a child could desire in the way of dressing-up clothes . . . there were cowboy outfits and Indian headdresses, Robin Hood clothes and a Davy Crockett set, a knight's helmet and shield, a fairy dress with wings and a wand.

The fairy dress belonged to Princess Anne and had been specially created for her by Norman Hartnell, the royal fashion designer. But Anne, as a child, was usually more tomboyish than fairylike and always preferred to join in the more robust games favoured by her big brother. She was often seen running about the palace with a pair of toy six-shooters strapped around her tiny waist, and one visitor to the royal nursery recalls a small, blonde apparition springing suddenly from around a corner, toy gun in hand, with a shrill cry of "Stick 'em up," a phrase presumably acquired from watching westerns on the children's television programmes.

A battered and much-used rocking horse which no longer boasted a tail added verisimilitude to nursery games of cowboys and Indians. It had belonged originally to the Queen and Princess Margaret, who knew it as Dapple. But that was before the era of television. Inherited by Charles and Anne, it was now, in turn, Champion the Wonder Horse and the Lone Ranger's talented mount, Silver. Royal children being no different from other children in the matter of playthings, it was perhaps not surprising that there should be the occasional childhood squabble over the right to ride this old and trusty favourite.

Joke novelties were another source of childhood fun. Visitors to the royal nursery were occasionally frightened—or at least *pretended* to be frightened—by a rather horrible and realistic-looking toy spider with furry legs and beady eyes which Prince Philip brought back for the children from one of his trips abroad. Some 'squeaking fruit' which he similarly brought back from a visit to the British Industries Fair one year provided its share of fun. So did a plate-wobbling gadget, operated by a rubber bulb at the end of a length of flexible tube. Another nursery novelty was a squeaking cushion . . . and there was an occasion at Sandringham when the Bishop of Norwich, having preached in the parish church of St. Mary Magdalene, was invited to Sandringham House afterwards for lunch with the Queen. After lunch, His Grace decided to rest briefly on a window seat affording a pleasant view of the royal grounds. It was a seat to which visitors to Sandringham habitually resorted, a fact not unknown to Prince Charles, and the Archbishop was in the very act of sitting down when a manservant rushed over and made a hurried pretence of re-arranging the cushions before making a discreet withdrawal with Charles' squeaking cushion now hidden behind his back.

Imitation ink had its victims, too, the Queen among them. She entered her sitting room on one occasion and was dismayed to see what was apparently a large stain of ink on the carpet. She was about to examine it more closely when half-suppressed giggles from behind one of the armchairs gave the game away. The giggles turned to boyish laughter as the Queen, entering into the spirit of the joke, took a piece of blotting paper from her desk and pretended to soak up the 'ink'.

Life in the royal nursery was further enlivened around this time by the arrival of two sprightly newcomers, Whisky and Sherry, destined very quickly to become world famous as the royal children's pet corgis. These nimble, fox-like little creatures have been firm favourites with the Royal Family since the Queen's father acquired the first of the line—nicknamed 'Dookie' in preference to his full title of Rozavel Golden Eagle—while still Duke of York. Prior to the arrival of Whisky and Sherry, there were already two corgis in residence at Buckingham Palace, Susan, a close favourite of the Queen until her death at Sandringham a year or so later, and Susan's daughter, Sugar.

It was Sugar, on one occasion, who was the subject of a small, hilarious misunderstanding in the royal nursery. The Queen was in her sitting room with the corgis when one of the royal footmen entered and asked if he could take Sugar upstairs to the nursery. The children wanted her, he said. The Queen agreed and Sugar was taken up to the nursery where Charles and Anne were sitting at the meal table.

"I've brought Sugar," said the footman.

A brief, puzzled silence was followed, almost immediately, by an outburst of laughter from the two children. The sugar they wanted was of the crystalline not canine, variety.

In due course, Sugar went to Windsor to have the puppies she was expecting and each weekend the two children would go along with their mother to visit her.

These weekends at Windsor provided a welcome diversion from palace life. There was so much more freedom to be savoured, so many new adventures to be experienced. There was the thrill of watching Papa play polo at Smith's Lawn and the fun of running on to the field between chukkas to help tread down the divots kicked up by the polo ponies. There were the Royal Farms with their animals ... horses, sheep, cattle. Such outings were not always without incident. Taken to watch sheep being dipped on one occasion, the small boy who was the future King ventured too close to the scene of operations and fell in. For one so young, it was an unpleasant and perhaps frightening experience and he was excusably in tears as he was hurried back to Windsor Castle for a hot bath and a change of clothing.

There was at this time no swimming pool at Windsor Castle. It was only in comparatively recent times that Queen Victoria's Orangery, under Prince Philip's direction, was converted to a modern, heated pool. But the fact that there was no pool did not prevent Charles and Anne taking a dip at weekends in warm weather. The fountain became a substitute swimming pool and there was one occasion at least, during an exceptionally hot week-end, when the uninhibited Prince Philip donned his own swimming trunks and joined them.

When Sugar had her puppies, the two children were given one

each to take back with them to Buckingham Palace. The new pets were each provided with a small, collapsible dog-bed in the nursery kitchen. Water-bowls from which they could refresh themselves when necessary were placed in the kitchen, the day nursery and the nursery corridor, and it was the children's responsibility to ensure that the bowls were kept filled.

Charles called his pet Whisky; Anne christened hers Sherry . . . and promptly proceeded to train it to perform a number of canine tricks. She taught it to jump through a child's hoop on the word 'Jump', to lie down and roll over across the nursery floor at the command 'Roll'.

"Ball," Anne would say and Sherry would immediately trot over to the toy cupboard, returning with a rubber ball in her mouth. Yet another of Sherry's tricks, bringing quiet applause from visitors to whom it was demonstrated, was to dart nimbly in and out between Anne's legs as she walked along.

II

In Britain, as elsewhere, it was a time of change. New ideas were springing up, new social attitudes developing. The scientist and the technician had replaced the local parson and the village policeman as people of importance in the community. It was the beginning of an era of affluence and the status symbols that go with it. And the pace of change was accelerating, bringing with it the need for a similar change in the concept of royal upbringing if the future King Charles III, when the time came for him to ascend the Throne, was not to prove merely a symbolic anachronism.

Any future monarch, if he was to be something more than a musty survival of ancient tradition, needed a far wider outlook, more advanced and at the same time more down to earth, than any of his predecessors had ever known. He need not have the training of a nuclear physicist, but he would require an understanding and appreciation of many things other than ship-launchings and tree-plantings and how to lay foundation stones. The palace schoolroom and a governess, with perhaps a succession of private tutors to follow, was no longer a sufficient education for a future monarch in a world where men were literally reaching for the moon.

Prince Philip saw this clearly even if no one else did at first.

An American scientist was to say of the Queen's husband some years later: "He does not know a great deal about science, but he knows enough to ask sensible questions and to be interested in the answers." But long before that was said Prince Philip had realised that his son, the future King, needed to be at least similarly equipped, and not only in the field of science. So began what was tantamount to a royal revolution.

Like most revolutions it had small beginnings. They took the form of an official announcement made in the Queen's name, but with Prince Philip's forward-looking attitudes plainly discernible in the background.

"Her Majesty and the Duke of Edinburgh have decided that their son has reached a stage when he should take part in more grown-up educational pursuits with other children."

It was the first tentative experimental step in a major royal change . . . a change which was to take Prince Charles, in due course, to day school and boarding school, to Gordonstoun and Timbertop, as the first heir to the Throne in Britain's long history to sit beside other boys in an ordinary classroom, to experience at first hand something of the give and take, the rough and tumble of ordinary life.

"In consequence," the official statement continued, "a certain amount of the Duke of Cornwall's instruction will take place outside his home; for example, he will attend classes and visit museums and other places of interest.

"The Queen trusts therefore that His Royal Highness will be able to enjoy this in the same way as other children can without the embarrassment of constant publicity.

"In this respect, Her Majesty feels it is equally important that those in charge of or sharing in the instruction should be spared undue publicity which can so seriously interrupt their normal lives."

Charles had in fact, by the time the announcement was issued, already sallied forth from the palace on one or two little publicised outings. There had been a day in March when Miss Peebles took him to the underground station at Trafalgar Square, where he bought tickets from a machine, rode down on the escalator and stood on the platform, an inconspicuous small boy with unruly hair, watching the electric trains come and go, emerging from and disappearing into tunnels just as they did on his working model of the Rock of Gibraltar.

There were, additionally, one or two more personal outings to a shop near Victoria Station, only a few hundred yards from his palace home, to spend his pocket money.

As we have shown, Prince Charles had been brought up from birth not to be spoiled on account of his unique position. Among other things, he was taught always to understand the value of money and not to imagine that it simply grew on trees. There was an occasion at Sandringham when he returned from a childhood outing with news that he had lost a new lead bought for one of the dogs. His mother reportedly inquired if he had looked for it and was told that he had but had been unable to find it. Then he must go back and have another look, the Queen is supposed to have said.

As a small boy, his pocket money was limited to two shillings and sixpence a week, with an additional grant to enable him to buy gifts for friends and relatives at Christmas time. Later this was increased to five shillings a week. But at either level, the difficulty was that there was nowhere to spend it except on those infrequent outings to the shop near Victoria Station. Mostly he saved it towards his summer holiday at Balmoral when he was permitted to go shopping in nearby Ballater.

From such childhood shopping expeditions, Charles, always a generous-hearted youngster, invariably returned with a paper bag containing three or four sixpenny bars of chocolate or candy—presents for members of the nursery staff and other royal servants he knew best.

But it was Anne, at an early age, who returned to Balmoral on one occasion with a most unusual gift. She was shopping in the small village store at Crathie when her eye lighted upon a packet of detergent. To the surprise of the shopkeeper, she added it to her small list of purchases. It was "a present for Nanny," she explained.

The royal announcement about Prince Charles' future produced the inevitable flurry of speculation. Palace spokesmen, in reply to inquiries from newspapers, said that if the young Prince should speak to anyone in the course of these instructional outings, as there was every likelihood that he would, the Queen desired that he should be answered as informally as any other youngster. She did not wish him to be addressed by his official title or shown any other special consideration. In short, she wanted him to be able to turn up at places like the Zoo, unheralded and unannounced, pay his money and walk quietly around like any other small boy, without any fanfare of trumpets, red carpet or official handshaking, without any eager, rubber-necking crowd following him everywhere, and a covey of newspaper photographers recording his every move.

If some people gained the idea that from then on they were likely to bump into the future King almost anywhere and everywhere, they were mistaken. What happened in practice was that Prince Charles, over a period of time, visited such places as the Science Museum, the Tower of London and Westminster Abbey. Later came visits to the waxworks at Madame Tussauds, the celestial panorama in the adjoining Planetarium and similar youthful outings.

Whether this was all that was visualised at the time of the original announcement is something only the boy's parents know. Certainly it was too much to hope that public enthusiasm would permit the future King to move about as freely as any ordinary youngster.

There was, at this period of royal life, a public adulation of the Queen, as a fresh and youthful monarch, of Prince Philip, as the real-life embodiment of the fairy prince on the white charger, and of their two young children—the slightly serious-faced Charles and the more extrovert Anne—such as never before in history. Nor was such adulation restricted merely to Britain and the Commonwealth. It was immediately and equally apparent in countries unconnected with either Crown or Commonwealth. It seemed that wherever she went the Queen was to be accorded the sort of frenzied, tumultuous, sensation-seeking welcome which an earlier generation had reserved for movie stars, and a later generation was to accord to a small group of pop singers. It was fostered, in part, by the image of a new Elizabethan age born of a young Queen, her athletic-looking husband and a couple of nice, likeable kids.

But its beginnings had their roots a couple of generations earlier. It started, in fact, with the Queen's grandparents, King George V and the regal Queen Mary. Until then, the Royal Family had kept largely out of the public eye. Queen Victoria, certainly after the death of her beloved Prince Albert, led an almost cloistered life. King Edward VII seldom put himself much on public display. But George V, when he ascended the Throne in turn, felt deeply that the Crown should be linked more closely with the people.

With this end in view, he and Queen Mary began a series of visits to mining villages in Wales and factories in England's industrial North. World War I brought an intensification of this contact between Crown and people with royal visits to war factories, troop camps, hospitals.

Yet even with the end of World War I Buckingham Palace was not yet the magnet it has become in more recent years. That was still in the future as the Royal Family pursued its course of drawing closer to the people. The people, in turn, responded with an adulation which reached fresh peaks at successive times of national sorrow and rejoicing. At times such as the birth of Prince Charles, Buckingham Palace became a focal point for public emotion, drawing people from miles. And a full week before Princess Anne was born it was estimated that as many as five thousand people an hour were filing past Clarence House.

It was a form of wholesale adoration from which it seemed there was no escape. Even in such a remote spot as the grounds of Abergeldie Castle there was something approaching a near-riot when the Queen and her family went there to help with a sale of work arranged to raise funds for Crathie parish church. It is a quiet, sparsely populated district. Yet such was the lure of Royalty that thousands flocked to the sale. Children were knocked over in the rush to buy the things the Royal Family were selling, women were jammed against the temporary crush barriers erected for the occasion and those unable to get in at the front of the marquee had no hesitation about going round to the back and ripping their way through the canvas for a glimpse of Royalty acting as salesmen and saleswomen. The sale had been planned to last for no more than two hours, but half-an-hour after that there was still no sign that the struggling, pushing mass of sightseers was in any way wearying. Little wonder that Princess Margaret, mopping her brow with her hand, gave vent to a heartfelt "Phew!"

The future King, his small sister helping him, dispensed postcards on that occasion. There was no shortage of purchasers. Charles was then, as he is now, the most famous boy in the world. Just as Anne was and is the most famous girl.

Ever since they were born, millions of acres of newsprint and millions of gallons of printer's ink have been devoted to recording their upbringing and adventures. Whatever they said or did has been published and read with enthusiasm in a score of countries. Anything they wore, particularly as youngsters, has been assiduously copied. There was a positive rash of small girls with white muffs after Anne was first seen with one. Sailor suits, deerstalker hats, tartan trews . . . all became freshly fashionable for small boys at varying times after Charles had been seen in them.

"Charles and Anne," said an official of the International Wool Secretariat around this time, "are the latest trend-setters on both sides of the Atlantic."

Amidst all this adulation and imitation, the Queen and her husband struggled diligently to retain their children's lives and upbringing on an even keel. Attempts to enrol Prince Charles and his small sister in juvenile or charitable organisations were politely but firmly discouraged. "There will be plenty of time for that later on," Prince Philip told a man who wanted to know why the two children were not on show at a palace garden party.

When official functions were held at the palace, the children,

65

though they were permitted to peep at the arrival of distinguished visitors, were never allowed to participate.

It was perhaps as well, for Charles, despite his royal training, was still of an age to speak with boy-like candour.

"Just look at that funny hat, Anne," he was heard to remark on one occasion as he and his sister watched official guests arriving at the palace from the vantage-point of an upstairs window.

6 *High Days and Holidays*

I

For Prince Charles, as for almost any other small boy, perhaps the happiest days at this early stage of his life were the holidays . . . the long stay at Sandringham over Christmas when breath steamed in the frosty air and snow covered fields and woods with a mantle of white, the long, lazy days of high summer amidst the vast hill and heather acres of Balmoral. Both places—Sandringham House and Balmoral Castle—are his mother's private property (not the property of the State) and will one day be his. Both are reasonably secluded, places where he could climb and race about and occasionally get grubby, as small boys will, without fear of the fact becoming public property.

Tough corduroy trousers and gaily-coloured sweaters were suitable clothing for such boyish pursuits, with a windcheater for extra warmth in cold weather. In Scotland, a miniature kilt made for novel variation upon occasion.

On holiday, away from Buckingham Palace and the nursery schoolroom, with comparative freedom to roam the hills and woods to his heart's content, much of the young Prince's customary solemnity would seem to vanish. While it was normally his small sister, Anne, who displayed the more extrovert personality, at holiday times, as though something inside him responded to fresh air and freedom, it seemed to be Prince Charles who always had most to say for himself, tales of boyish adventure to relate, at the end of a day spent in the open.

Outdoor pursuits left him occasionally grubby and always tousle-haired, and it was a standing instruction that both he and Anne must wash thoroughly, change their clothes and tidy their hair before sitting down to meals. Childhood appetites, sharpened by fresh air and exercise, may well have caused both children to ignore this parental edict upon occasion, and a former royal servant has revealed in an interview published in a Continental magazine that once, at least, the Queen surprised her small daughter in the act of scoffing cakes without having gone through the customary preliminaries. The Princess was rebuked by her mother and sent to her room to wash and change.

The same source reveals that both children, from an early age, were trained to help themselves from dishes which the servants brought round at mealtimes. Prince Charles, like any other healthy youngster, always seemed to be ravenously hungry and would sometimes heap his plate too full. The Queen was quick to correct him on such occasions. "That's enough, Charles," she would say, adding that he could have more when he had finished what was already on his plate.

At Balmoral, when the weather was too inclement for outdoor pursuits, the kitchen became a favourite play-place for the royal youngsters. There was the twofold attraction of helping the chefs, and helping themselves to any tasty titbits that were going. At least, Anne seems to have helped herself. The less uninhibited Charles would usually ask first if he could have some of whatever was going.

Charles Mellis, formerly head chef on the royal train, tells of how the two children visited him in his diminutive travelling kitchen on one occasion as the train journeyed north to Scotland through the night. He was busy at the time preparing a batch of what restaurants know as 'French fried potatoes' and the rest of us refer to as 'chips'. Anne promptly helped herself to a handful and began munching. But not Charles. He looked at Mellis and asked, politely, "May I have some too, please, chef?" Of course, he got them.

At Balmoral, on wet days, the two children would spend long hours in the kitchen. They loved to help with the baking of tea-cakes and biscuits and with the preparation of salads. Sometimes they would go through to the cold-meat larder to watch one of the kitchen porters pluck the grouse with nimble fingers. Occasionally, if there was trout on the menu, they would be allowed to net the live fish swimming in the fish-tank. Most enjoyable of all was helping to make the ice-cream . . . real creamy ice-cream . . . and sampling the different flavours they had helped to make, vanilla, coffee and chocolate.

"We've come to help," they would announce to the head chef, Yorkshire-born Ronald Aubrey, upon arrival at the kitchen. "What can we do today?"

Usually he found something to occupy their willing fingers, if it was only to fetch fresh supplies from the larder. There is a story which has the ring of probability about it that there was one occasion on which he asked them to fetch him some fresh eggs. They were on their way back from the supply store, climbing the flight of granite steps which leads to the kitchen, carrying the eggs in a basin, when there was a sudden crash followed by the sound of childish voices raised in recrimination one against the other. A moment later Charles burst into the kitchen with news that they had broken the eggs but would willingly go back for some more.

When they tired of helping out in the kitchen they would make their way back to the nursery. On their way back they usually popped into the coffee room, knowing that they could always charm the maid into giving them chocolate biscuits for themselves and sugar lumps for their ponies.

It was during one of these frequent expeditions to the kitchen that Prince Charles heard the ping-pong of a ball from inside the silver pantry. Always of an inquiring nature, he opened the door and looked in. Two members of the staff, during their time off, were playing table tennis. Boy-like, Charles asked them to show him how to play.

They showed him how to hold a bat and taught him the rudiments of the game. For weeks after, whenever his mother or nanny wanted him for any reason, they knew where to look for him. Invariably he was either in the silver pantry or in the staff recreation room, playing table tennis with footmen, butlers, pages or chefs, whoever he could persuade to give him a game. For one so young, he became considerably adept. Whenever the ball went under the table, as it did frequently, he would dive to retrieve it with such eagerness that he often emerged with one hand clutching the ball, the other caressing his tousled head.

"I've hit my head," he would say, "but it doesn't hurt."

Royal servants, his small sister, his father ... these were his customary companions, though occasionally, and more especially later when schooldays began and he formed his own friendships, there were boys of his own age. Early companions during these summer holidays at Balmoral were his German cousins, the children of Prince Philip's youngest sister, Princess Sophie, and her husband, Prince George of Hanover. Guelf, the oldest of the three German youngsters, was a year older than Prince Charles. Then there was George, a year younger, and their small sister, Frederika-Elizabeth, some three years younger than Princess Anne.

In fine weather, their parents allowed the hardy German youngsters to race barefooted along the paths and lawns at Balmoral, clad in diminutive swim-trunks, their bodies exposed to the sun. Of course, Charles and Anne begged to do the same and the fountain in the rose-garden became a favourite play-place for all five youngsters when the weather was really warm.

Picnics high in the heather-clad hills or on the shores of Loch Muick formed a regular part of holiday life at Balmoral. Nor were these any ordinary picnics of dog-eared sandwiches and crumbling cake. Long before the rest of Britain awoke to the fact that outdoor meals need not necessarily be makeshift, Prince Philip had a portable barbecue outfit he would take along with him on such occasions with the whole family joining cheerfully in the preparation of the picnic meal. Later, during the royal tour of Canada in 1957, he was driving along with the Queen in one of the royal cars when his quick eyes spotted a more elaborate barbecue kit in a shop window they were passing. He sent a member of his staff to make inquiries, found out that it was fitted with an automatic spit for turning meat and bought it.

Prince Charles thoroughly enjoyed these barbecue picnics. First thing in the morning he would go along to the kitchen with his father and help in selecting the food—steak or chops, sausages or chicken—for the day's outing. Food, barbecue and the other requisites of outdoor life were loaded into a Land Rover and off they would go. If they were heading for Loch Muick, fishing rods would be strapped to the roof of the vehicle for Charles and his father to cast for trout. Sometimes Anne, always eager to copy whatever Charles did, would join in, too. If the catch consisted of only one or two small trout, they would clean and barbecue the fish on the spot. Other times they would take their catch back to Balmoral with them and ask the chef if he would cook it for either their supper or their breakfast.

As they grew bigger, tricycles were replaced by bicycles for the royal youngsters and sometimes, by way of a change, they would follow the Land Rover in which their parents rode under their own pedal-power. On one such outing, with Anne too tired to cycle back to Balmoral at the end of the day, her father volunteered to ride her bicycle back for her.

The Land Rover containing the rest of the royal party had been back at Balmoral some considerable time before Prince Philip finally put in an appearance—on foot, with Anne's bicycle hoisted across his shoulders. It appeared that the combination of his stalwart frame and the rough surface of one Highland track he had had to negotiate had proved too much for Anne's small-framed bicycle and it had buckled beneath him.

Especially exciting to Prince Charles around this time were the, to him, highly adventurous overnight excursions on which he and his father occasionally embarked. Anne usually went along, too, on such outings, though the Queen, doubtless at her own wish, preferred to remain behind in the more comfortable surroundings of her Highland home. But for a youngster like Charles, comfort was easily outweighed by the prospect of a night spent in the great outdoors. He and his father would load the Land Rover with food, barbecue equipment, fishing rods, sleeping-bags and whatever else they might require and set off into the hills, heading usually for a secluded spot along the shores of Loch Muick where they could swim, fish and cook their own meals before spending the night rolled in their sleeping-bags in a seldom-used shooting lodge.

It was around this time, too, that Prince Philip conceived the idea of constructing a scale model of Balmoral Castle with its *schloss*-like turrets and dominating clock tower. One can easily imagine with what high degree of boyish enthusiasm Prince

Charles, always a clever youngster with his hands, hailed this paternal project, tagging along with his father while he took photographs of the castle from every angle. Developed and printed, the photographs formed the basis for the constructional plan. Section by section, bent over a work-table in his study, Prince Philip began to construct a scale model of the castle which was to be complete down to the smallest detail . . . even to chimney pots, door knobs and a flagpole. As the model, over a period of some years, gradually outgrew the study in size and convenience, he transferred his efforts to a ground-floor room which he had converted into a workshop complete with bench, vice, electric drill and electrically operated saw.

A winding granite staircase climbs the flag tower at Balmoral, leading to the clock mechanism and the open parapet where the royal standard flies when the Queen is in residence. One day, in company with Prince William of Gloucester and Prince Michael of Kent, Prince Charles embarked upon another of his boyhood journeys of exploration. Princess Anne, of course, had to go along, too. All four youngsters were engrossed in some game which involved running up and down the stairs and racing round the flagpole on the roof when it was realised what they were about. They were hurriedly summoned down to ground level again and strict instructions were given for the door at the top of the tower to be kept locked for the future.

Similar instructions were issued at Windsor Castle after a fire exit leading on to the roof at the top of the Queen's Tower was discovered ajar one day. Charles and Anne had spotted the door, decided to investigate further, and were actually out on the open roof, playing a risky game of hide-and-seek among the skylights, chimney pots and battlements, with a drop of 100 feet or more to the ground below, when their absence was noticed and they were tracked down. After that, the fire exit was always kept locked on the Queen's instructions with the key kept close to hand, but hung where the two youngsters could not reach it.

It will be gathered from all this that the future King and his small sister were no different from any other youngsters during those inquisitive, adventurous years of early childhood; no better

—and certainly no worse. By virtue of his environment, Prince Charles perhaps had fewer opportunities than ordinary youngsters for becoming grubby and getting into scrapes, but when opportunity presented itself his sturdy, inquiring, boyish nature was by no means backward in taking advantage of the fact.

At this stage of their young lives, the two children, Charles and Anne, were well-nigh inseparable. Basically unlike each other in so many ways, they were yet close friends and real companions. As they grew, so the differences in their natures were accentuated. Prince Charles, boyish though he was, was also cautious in many things, quiet, extremely patient and painstakingly methodical in whatever he undertook. Princess Anne, on the other hand, seemed always restless, short on patience, seldom silent and never still for more than a few seconds at a time.

The basic difference in their two characters was clearly seen the time they were each given a child's painting-by-numbers outfit. Charles, patient and painstaking as well as artistically inclined, plugged away steadily until an extremely creditable landscape painting was the result. Anne, by contrast, found the exercise extremely tedious and never completed her painting.

II

Summer cruises aboard the royal yacht *Britannia* provided Prince Charles with further opportunities to try his sea-legs. "I wish I could go on the yacht again," he had said more than once following the voyage to Tobruk. Now he got his wish.

During the first of these summer holiday cruises the yacht served also as a floating base from which the Queen and Prince Philip paid official visits to the Isle of Man and to various places in Wales. It was while the yacht was anchored off the Welsh coast that the future Prince of Wales set foot in his Principality for the first time, being carried ashore from the royal barge for a family picnic which also included the fun of paddling in rock pools and investigating the lobster pots of local fishermen.

For the most part, the yacht steamed by night and anchored by day while the Royal Family picnicked ashore in some quiet cove.

PRINCE CHARLES

Fishing from the shore in company with his father provided additional amusement for the young Prince. Even more exciting were trips in the speedboat, Prince Philip at the helm, the sea foaming away behind them as they circled the royal yacht.

Another shore visit took Charles and Anne to have tea with Granny Queen Mother at the Castle of Mey, which she had recently acquired and renovated as a secluded, away-from-it-all retreat amidst the moors of Caithness, Britain's most northerly county.

But the excitement of going ashore even to see their beloved Granny was nothing compared with the excitement the two children displayed when they went back aboard *Britannia* again. The reason for their excitement lay in the fact that Granny had promised them a very special 'surprise' treat and their parents had agreed that they could stay up a little later than usual in order to enjoy it. After supper, wearing pyjamas and dressing gowns, Charles and Anne went back on deck as *Britannia* set sail again.

Shorewards, the ancient battlements of Granny's castle were silhouetted against a darkening sky. One can imagine with what childhood anticipation the two youngsters awaited what followed. Suddenly, from the castle battlements, a rocket soared upwards to burst with startling brilliance against the night sky. Then another ... and another ... while on shore a bonfire burst into flame, blazing in the darkness as a focal point for the firework display which was Granny's surprise treat for her small grandchildren.

On one of these summer cruises aboard the royal yacht Charles took Chi-Chi along with him. Chi-Chi, a golden hamster, had been given to him to divert his young mind from the sad passing of Harvey, his pet rabbit. The boy had become extremely attached to his new pet and would frequently have him out of his cage to play with him, sometimes to his mother's consternation. Fond though she is of most animals, and especially of horses and dogs, the Queen could arouse little enthusiasm for her small son's rodent-like pet.

One day, aboard *Britannia*, Chi-Chi was out of his cage when he eluded the hands of his young master, scurried across the vessel's sun-lounge and took refuge behind the built-in radiogram. In vain Charles tried to tempt him out again with tasty titbits.

At bedtime, with still no sign of Chi-Chi, Charles carried the

74

hamster's cage into the sun-lounge and left it in front of the radiogram, the door open and a supply of fresh food inside. But the following morning the cage was still empty. Either Chi-Chi was well content where he was or he was quite unable to find his way out of the labyrinth of wires into which he had ventured. There was only one thing to do and the yacht's radio mechanic was summoned to dismantle the set. And there was Chi-Chi, comfortably curled up, fast asleep, as snug as . . . well, as a hamster in a radiogram.

Prince Charles himself caused considerable consternation, at least among those members of the royal staff who knew of the incident, the day he disappeared aboard the royal yacht. He had been playing hide-and-seek with Prince Michael of Kent and had somehow hidden himself so well that neither Michael nor anyone else could find him.

Anxious to avoid alarming the boy's mother, members of the royal staff organised a quick search of the yacht and a member of the search party has related in a Continental magazine how he heard faint scratching sounds coming from the built-in wardrobe in Prince Michael's cabin.

He went over to the wardrobe and opened it and out tumbled the future King, red-faced from the stuffiness of his hiding place and perhaps not a little frightened. He had, it seems, climbed into the wardrobe to hide, pulling the door shut behind him. When no one came to find him he had tried to let himself out again—to find himself trapped by a door which opened only from the outside!

III

Sandringham, like Balmoral, offered an almost endless variety of adventures and pursuits dear to the heart of a growing boy . . . woods and fields, farms and stables. Perhaps more than anything else, Prince Charles, at this stage of his life, enjoyed being out in the shooting field, watching his father head a party of guns, joining with the beaters as they drove the pheasants, helping to count the bag at the end of a day's shooting.

His small sister was usually with him on such occasions. But whereas Charles, even at this young age, took the whole business of shooting game-birds with masculine seriousness, the irrepressible Anne was constantly teasing and larking about. A former gamekeeper at Sandringham recalls one occasion when Charles was trying to count the day's bag and Anne was constantly interrupting.

Finally, Charles became exasperated with these juvenile antics. "Do be quiet, Anne," he remonstrated. "I'm counting."

"When you count," his sister teased in reply, "your hair stands on end."

Both youngsters loved to beg a ride in the game cart when the shooting party moved on from one area to the next. One day, as they rode in the game cart, Anne noticed a curious bundle securely knotted inside a large, coloured handkerchief.

"What's that?" she wanted to know.

"They're my elevenses," the driver of the game cart informed her in his sing-song Norfolk accent.

Anne, of course, had no idea what 'elevenses' were and at lunchtime she watched, fascinated, as the driver unknotted the coloured handkerchief and produced a makeshift meal of thickly cut sandwiches and a large wedge of home-baked cake, quite different from the paper-thin sandwiches and dainty tea-cakes to which the royal children were accustomed at Buckingham Palace.

"Can I have some?" Anne wanted to know as the driver settled down to his midday meal.

"Of course," said the driver, and happily and hungrily the small Princess shared his 'elevenses' with him.

For adult members of the shooting parties at Sandringham, lunch was invariably a more substantial affair. Sometimes they ate, picnic-fashion, in the open air, but more often in some suitably sheltered spot such as the village hall at Anmer or the little-used royal waiting room at Wolferton station.

In those days, with Charles not yet old enough to handle a gun of his own, he would stay behind with his mother when his father and the other members of the shooting party set off after breakfast. For the Queen, even though she might be at Sandringham and technically on holiday, there were always the contents of her leather-covered state boxes to be dealt with, official papers to be read, studied and signed, before she was free to enjoy the remainder of the day. This task done, she and the children would join the others of the shooting party for lunch and stay to watch the rest of the day's shooting.

The two youngsters usually finished their lunch in double-quick time and were off to play again. One day, at Wolferton, with lunch over and the rest of the shooting party about to move off, it was suddenly realised that there was no sign of the children.

A search had been in progress for some minutes when attention was attracted by a succession of shrill blasts from the whistle of a goods train loading sugar-beet in a neighbouring siding. Investigation revealed that Charles and Anne had been helped on to the footplate by a friendly engine-driver and were having the time of their lives playing 'trains'.

Royal children being no different from any other children, this was not the only occasion when childhood games and ideas caused them to disappear. There was, later, another occasion, this time at Balmoral, when they were nowhere to be found. Then it was noticed that their bicycles had gone, too. A detective mounted a bicycle and set off to look for them. He found them eventually in the church hall at Crathie, some distance from Balmoral Castle, happily helping with the preparations for a church sale-of-work.

At Sandringham, one of Charles' favourite play-places was the estate fire station. As a small boy, he was fascinated by the shiny red fire-engine and the gleaming helmets worn by the firemen. Whenever he could, he would make his way to the fire station . . . with Anne invariably tagging along with him.

"Can I have a helmet to put on, please?" he would ask.

The firemen would give him one. It was rather too big for him, of course, and came down almost over his eyes. Unperturbed, he would clamber up on to the fire-engine, sit in the driver's seat and grip the wheel in his hands. Anne, of course, would climb up beside him.

"Fire! Fire!" Charles would call out, pretending to drive to the scene of an imaginary blaze while Anne, sitting alongside, clanged the alarm bell noisily to clear the way ahead.

In the unfortunate event that Sandringham House should ever

catch fire, it would take more than the estate's small fire brigade to quell the resulting blaze, and from time to time firemen from all parts of Norfolk converge on the Queen's country home for a practice drill. Charles loved these fire drills . . . the clanging of alarm bells, the roar of the fire-engines as they rushed through the gates and up to the house, the uncoiling of the hoses, the turntable ladders being brought into operation.

With his mother keeping a watchful eye on him, he would pick his way among the gleaming fire appliances and gushing hoses, gazing with admiration at the firemen in their shining helmets.

"May I turn the water on, please?" he asked the crew of one fire pump and was almost beside himself with boyish delight when they let him.

During one of these practice drills there was, for the young Prince, the additional thrill of being helped out of the nursery window to slide down a rescue chute into the burly arms of firemen waiting to catch him at the bottom.

Such was his boyish charm that he had little difficulty in persuading people to do almost anything for him. Once he persuaded a policeman on duty in the grounds of Sandringham House to lend him his helmet and truncheon for a boyhood game of 'cops and robbers'. Taken to Wolferton station to say goodbye to some relatives who had been staying with his parents at Sandringham, he charmed the stationmaster into giving him a whistle and a green flag so that he could signal the train on its way. It left for London that day three minutes late and the whistle the future King had used to signal it out was hung in a place of honour in the stationmaster's office against the possibility that he might want to use it again on some future occasion.

IV

Christmas was a particularly exciting time of year at Sandringham . . . and doubly exciting those years when woods and fields were covered with a deep, crisp mantle of snow. There was one year around this time when the weather was unusually cold and hard, with the snow even crisper and deeper than usual.

Helped by their nanny, Charles and Anne built a big snowman in front of the house, positioning it where they could keep an eye on it from the nursery windows.

Pieces of coal provided the snowman with bright, beady eyes. The royal youngsters begged or borrowed an old bowler hat to perch on his head. A man's pipe they got from somewhere completed the effect.

The cold weather lasted a long time that particular Christmas and some six weeks later the snowman was still standing there, looking up at the nursery windows with his unwinking, coal-black eyes.

Snowball fights in which Papa—and sometimes Mummy— joined made for additional fun. Prince Philip walked out of the main door at Sandringham House one snowy winter's day to find his young son pelting snowballs at a patrolling policeman. Quite obviously, the poor policeman did not know quite how to cope with this furious snowball attack on the part of the future monarch.

But Prince Philip had no such doubts.

"Don't just stand there, man," he called out. "Throw some back."

Among the gifts Charles and Anne received one Christmas were two novel toboggans in the shape of flying saucers. They took their new toboggans out on to the terrace at Sandringham, where their father and some of the staff took it in turns to send them shooting off down the long snow-covered slope.

The two royal youngsters soon discovered that they could make the toboggans spin round and round in circles as they plunged down the slippery slope. Finally, Charles made his spin so violently that it turned right over, unseating him and plunging him into the snow.

The year Charles was six, he was taken, as a childhood treat, to a London store to see its Palace of Toys and meet Father Christmas. Of course, it wasn't really Father Christmas. It was the store's chief commissionaire disguised with a red robe and a nylon beard. At this time, the young Prince still believed in Father Christmas. But doubts were perhaps beginning to creep into his inquiring young mind.

"Do sleighs really fly?" he wanted to know.

"Of course they do," the muffled voice from behind the nylon beard assured him.

"Then *how* do they fly?" Charles demanded.

Father Christmas obviously considered it was high time to change the subject.

"Tell me what you want for Christmas," he suggested.

About that, at least, Charles was in no doubt.

"A bicycle, please," he said, eagerly.

He took Santa's hand in his and dragged him across to where a shiny red bicycle was on display.

"A red one—this one."

"I'll make a special note of it," Santa assured him.

Charles believed in Father Christmas up until the time he started school. But one thing always puzzled him.

"If Father Christmas comes down the nursery chimney, why doesn't the fire burn him?" he wanted to know.

Later, when he came to realise that there was no such person as Father Christmas, he was at some pains to ensure that Anne did not find out.

"We musn't let Anne know there isn't a Father Christmas or it will spoil things for her," he confided in the staff of the royal nursery.

In due course, Anne was to find out, too. But by that time there was another addition to the Royal Family, a baby brother named Andrew, with Charles and Anne conspiring to keep the truth from him for as long as possible.

Each year, as Christmas drew near, Charles, as part of his lessons in the nursery schoolroom, would draw or colour his own Christmas cards to send to Mummy and Papa, Granny and Margo, Nanny Lightbody, Mamba (Miss Anderson) and Mispy (Miss Peebles). Charles, with his rather artistic nature, enjoyed the task, but Anne, when she came to join him for lessons in the schoolroom, was perhaps less enthusiastic.

"Why can't we buy Christmas cards instead of painting our own?" she is said to have grumbled on one occasion. "Everyone else does."

PHOTOGRAPH BY CECIL BEATON
CAMERA PRESS

Left. A charming study of the future king, nearing his second birthday with his month-old sister, Princess Anne.

A chubby determined Prince Charles clutches his mother's pearl entwined finger, as a smiling mother and proud father pose for their first picture with their baby son.

PHOTOGRAPH BY BARON
CAMERA PRESS

On his third birthday in November 1951, Prince Charles went to Buckingham Palace to see "Granny and Grandpapa". This photograph of him with the late King George VI was the last time they were pictured together. The King died less than three months later.

The Queen Mother with her small grandson at the Coronation.
Another charming study by Cecil Beaton.

An early public appearance. The future King, with his parents and baby sister,

"Oh dear," Prince Charles seems to be sighing as he leaves the aircraft that will take his father on a round-the-world tour, "Now I'm the man of the family and must look after things."

A boyhood study of the Prince, in a grey suit with a red tie, taken by the young photographer who is now Lord Snowdon.

KEYSTONE PRESS

Prince Charles, newly-created the Prince of Wales only 24 hours before this picture was taken, returns to Cheam School after attending morning service in the parish church. *Below.* A sturdy Prince dismantles a mock gun with schoolboy friends during a field day at Hill House.

KEYSTONE PRESS

"That was your father's room," Capt. Iain Tennant, chairman of the Board of governors, seems to be saying as he shows Prince Charles around on his first day at Gordonstoun.

Home from Cheam, Prince Charles plays with his baby brother, little Prince Andrew.

Prince Charles and Princess Anne photographed by Lord Snowdon in the Picture Gallery at Buckingham Palace. Anne is wearing a dress of white broderie with a blue sash and necklet of pearls on a platinum chain.

Both children looked forward eagerly to the annual Christmas visit to Sandringham . . . rushing through the frosty countryside in the royal train, and then a car ride in gathering darkness along three miles of road hemmed in by tall trees to where the lighted windows of Sandringham House beckoned a welcome.

Christmas preparations were usually in full swing when they arrived, with a bunch of mistletoe hanging in the front hall and red-berried holly adorning the main rooms.

With a small boy, first things come first. For Charles, one of the first things was to slip out of the nursery, run across the corridor and open the door leading on to the balcony which overlooks the ballroom, his eyes widening with delight as they took in the huge Christmas tree, bright with fairy lights, its topmost branches so near he could almost touch them from the balcony, its tip brushing the intricately moulded ceiling.

The ballroom balcony also offered him an opportunity for boyish pranks. Among his playthings, as a small boy, was a stuffed monkey, taller than he was himself at that time.

One day he crept unnoticed into the balcony, taking his toy monkey with him. He peeped over the edge. Down below two of the maids were busy with the dusting.

With a loud cry, Charles hurled his toy monkey over the balcony.

The maids looked up, saw what they took to be a human body crashing down on to the ballroom floor, let out a loud scream and fled for help.

On Christmas Eve, then as now, the ballroom became a focal point for family festivities as everyone slipped in and out with gaily wrapped parcels, adding to the piles on the cloth-covered tables set up around the Christmas tree. Each pile had its own card bearing the name of the fortunate recipient and, inevitably, the piles labelled Charles and Anne grew biggest of all.

But when the time came to open the gifts, poor Charles, like many another small boy, frequently suffered the humiliation of having to stand idly by while the grown-ups of the party played with his new toys under the thin pretence of showing him 'how they work'.

There was one boyhood Christmas when his gifts included a

81

miniature drum kit. But he could hardly get to play it. Everyone—Papa included—wanted to show how well they could emulate Gene Krupa and Joe Daniels.

Much the same sort of thing happened with a remote-control toy car which was a gift from Earl Mountbatten of Burma. For a long time Charles had to be content with simply looking on while his elders and betters demonstrated the correct technique for manoeuvring it under chairs and tables and round the big Christmas tree.

An electric train set, another Christmas, came in for the same treatment. Everyone earnestly assured him that he might break it if he tried to operate it himself, though that, as all small boys will know, was only a grown-up excuse to enable his father, the Duke of Gloucester and Billy Wallace, who was staying at Sandringham with the Royal Family at the time, to play with it themselves.

No wonder the young Prince was up and about at almost the crack of dawn the following morning. Asked where he was going, he said he wanted to play with his train set and reportedly added the gloomy proviso, "If it isn't worn out already."

The ballroom at Sandringham on Christmas Eve was also the venue for the small annual ceremony at which the Queen and Prince Philip distribute Christmas gifts to members of their staff. Charles, at this time, was not yet old enough to help his parents in the task of distribution, but he still shared in the general excitement, trotting round among the waiting recipients with such eager boyish questions as, "What are you getting this year . . . do you know what it is?"

He was as familiar with the staff at Sandringham as at Buckingham Palace and his questions, as he mingled with them, reflected the maturity of his outlook.

"Are there a lot of pheasants this year?" he would perhaps ask the head gamekeeper. Or, addressing himself to the kennel-man, "How are the dogs? I must come and see them."

Although personal gifts among the Queen and her family are always exchanged on Christmas Eve, some of those for Charles and Anne, when they were this age, were held back for delivery by Father Christmas, whichever of Sandringham's many chimneys he might clamber down in the night. Usually it was the Queen—though sometimes Prince Philip took over—who slipped into the children's bedrooms late at night to leave these held-over gifts at the foot of their beds along with the home-made stockings filled with fruit and nuts and candy and novelties. Anne's stocking, at this stage, usually contained a china miniature or two, while Charles, when he opened his so eagerly on Christmas morning, was always sure to find one or more miniature cars to add to his collection.

To the Queen, Christmas is not merely a time for feasting and presents and merry-making. She is conscious, above all else, of the religious significance of the occasion. On Christmas morning she always rises early to attend Holy Communion. Eleven o'clock finds her back in church for morning service. Charles had already been several times to the tiny church in the grounds of Royal Lodge at Windsor, and now, on Christmas morning at Sandringham, clutching a white prayer-book which was a gift from Granny, he went with his parents to the church of St. Mary Magdalene.

For the Royal Family, Christmas lunch was—and still is—followed by a 'breather' in the fresh air. For the menfolk, this usually takes the form of a brief stroll across to the kennels to look at the dogs and a chat with the head gamekeeper concerning shooting prospects. The ladies of the party go off elsewhere, often for a short car drive, with the children.

As a small boy, Charles went with his mother in the car. Then came the Christmas when the men were about to set off for the kennels and his father turned and said, "I think you might come with us, Charles."

It is not difficult to picture the young Prince's inner excitement as, hands clasped behind his back in the familiar royal attitude, he strolled across the grounds towards the kennels with his father and the other menfolk.

That year he must have felt that at last he had really begun to grow up.

7 *Prince Philip Looks Ahead*

I

It was Christmas, 1956. Prince Charles was now eight years old, and, as birthday photographs taken by Lord Snowdon (then still Tony Armstrong-Jones) showed, sturdy with it. But at eight, he was also of an age to need his father's company . . . and Prince Philip, that Christmas, was away aboard the royal yacht, bearded and duffle-coated, as he undertook a long and arduous tour of isolated communities and lonely survey posts as far south as the Antarctic, places the Queen, with the best will in the world, could not possibly fit into her own feminine itinerary.

Charles added his greeting of "Hello, Papa . . . a merry Christmas" to a recording his mother made to send out to Prince Philip for him to play back on Christmas Day. So did Princess Anne, and even the excited yapping of the pet corgis was recorded to provide an intimate, homely link of familiar sounds in Philip's cabin aboard the royal yacht. And on Christmas afternoon, at Sandringham House, the young Prince stood beside his mother in her sitting room as his father's voice came crackling by radio-telephone across the thousands of miles of ocean which lay between them.

But for a boy of eight, Christmas without his father was not quite the same and to offset the lack of fatherly companionship for him the Queen engaged a tutor to be with him at Sandringham in the weeks which followed Christmas. Her choice fell upon Mr. Michael Farebrother, a man of roughly Prince Philip's own age, a former Guards officer who was now headmaster of a preparatory school in Sussex. The two of them, the young Prince and his tutor, roamed the fields and woods of Sandringham together in a companionable relationship which did not, of course, entirely compensate for the absence of the boy's father. Sometimes they walked; sometimes they rode on bicycles, with

Charles on one occasion demonstrating his latest cycling trick.

"Look," he called out, sailing past his tutor as they cycled together in the grounds of Sandringham. "No hands."

Mr. Farebrother's presence at Sandringham was also a forerunner of a big and, by royal standards, drastic change in the upbringing of the future King . . . schooldays.

For generations past, private tutors had been the order of the day for children of the Royal Family. Tutors were hired and fired with almost clockwork regularity as Prince Albert devoted himself to the task of moulding the future Edward VII in his own industrious, painstaking image. His efforts, as it turned out, were largely in vain. Queen Victoria, before that, had been educated and trained by her mother and the Baroness Lehzen. Quite inadequately. George V also had private tutors and considered the same sort of upbringing sufficiently suitable for his sons. Suggestions that they should go at least to a private school for a time met with a firm rebuff based on the premise that what was good enough for their father was good enough for them. "My brother and I never went to a preparatory school," George V informed his sons gruffly.

So apart from brief spells in the naval colleges of Osborne and Dartmouth, the Duke of Windsor and his brother who became King George VI never went to school either. They, too, had a tutor, a man picked more for his qualities as a country gentleman than for his academic ability. When they failed, not unnaturally, to make as rapid progress as their father wished, additional tutors were hired to cram French, German and mathematics into them. True, they did go to university for a time, but while there they were still hemmed in by private tutors and shielded as far as possible from any undignified contact with undergraduates of less regal status.

King George VI, seemingly aware of the inadequacy of his own education, talked at one time about the possibility of sending his elder daughter, Princess Elizabeth, to school. But that was before he became King on his brother's abdication, with his daughter the future Queen. Once he found himself on the Throne, the plan for schooling was forgotten and the future Queen's education continued under the jurisdiction of her governess, Marion Crawford, with lessons in constitutional history from the late Sir Henry Marten, vice provost of Eton, and training in monarchy from her father himself.

Until now, Prince Charles' lessons had been similarly confined to the palace schoolroom and the good offices of his governess, Katherine Peebles. Initially, his lessons in English and arithmetic, history and geography, scripture and art, had lasted only until lunchtime. But now they extended to a full day with Anne providing scholastic company until lunchtime. A small desk had been introduced into the schoolroom for Anne's use with Charles still sitting at a table and Miss Peebles conducting lessons from behind her mahogany writing desk. In addition to the world globe, which served as a useful accessory for geography lessons, a large atlas on one wall was marked with the various overseas tours undertaken by the royal parents. For the two children, when their parents were away, geography was made to live with the use of pins and coloured thread to plot the progress of each new royal tour.

Despite the occasional and inevitable squabbles of childhood, the two youngsters remained close friends and constant companions, indoors and out. Youthful pranks and practical jokes still enlivened nursery life from time to time. A gift of some Mexican jumping beans was a cause of considerable hilarity. Charles was so enthused with his share of the beans that he insisted upon taking them to bed with him at night. But the beans, in their metal container, made such a racket in the quietness of night that they kept him awake and had to be removed.

Out of doors on fine days, a miniature caravan was an additional venue for childhood games. Parked close to the climbing frame and children's sandpit in the palace gardens, furnished with table, chairs and a china closet as well as an imitation sink and cooker, it was just big enough for grown-ups to enter if they ducked their heads sufficiently. But mostly Charles and Anne had it to themselves, a private world of childhood make-believe to which they took cups and plates and cutlery from the nursery for picnic meals which Anne pretended to cook for them on the diminutive cooker.

II

There was, at this time, a not inconsiderable amount of public controversy on the subject of the future King's upbringing. So much so, indeed, that the Queen and Prince Philip must sometimes have wondered who were their son's parents . . . they themselves or all the others who seemed to imagine that they knew far better than his mother and father what was best for him.

On all sides, advice was being constantly showered on them. *Get That Child A Haircut* thundered one headline in reference to the boy's Beatle-like hairstyle. *Are We Coddling The Prince?* another newspaper demanded with reference to his rather chubby outline. And Charles was still not yet ten when one newspaper writer, with seeming seriousness, was diligently discussing the question of future marriage and propounding a short list of eligible young ladies, ranging from the eight-year-old daughter of the Duke of Northumberland to the young Danish princess, then only eleven, who is now Queen of Greece.

Nor was such proxy parenthood by any means restricted to the newspapers. Letters of advice were constantly reaching the palace from all quarters of the world. For Charles to develop the slightest cough or cold was sufficient to attract a positive avalanche of letters advising various forms of treatment and even packages of cure-alls ranging from paper spills containing herb tea to camphor bags to be worn round the neck.

The question of the young Prince's future education aroused more controversy than anything else, and not only in Britain. Canadians advocated that he should be educated in Canada. Australians thought he should be educated in Australia. There was even one suggestion that his schooling should shift annually from place to place throughout the Commonwealth.

At home, private tutors, because of the special qualities required in a future King, were not without their advocates. But there were many other suggestions for schooling, each with its staunch band of supporters. Some people, Lady Pakenham among them, visualised Charles as going first to some small village school and then to a state-run school. Lord Altrincham had somewhat similar ideas.

"But will she [the Queen] have the wisdom to give her children an education very different from her own?" he asked in an article in the *National & English Review* which was to raise a deal of comment and controversy. "Will she, above all, see to it that Prince Charles is equipped with all the knowledge he can absorb without injury to his health, and that he mixes during his formative years with children who will one day be bus-drivers, dockers, engineers, etc.—not merely with future landowners or stockbrokers?"

The 'stop coddling' element, had they but been aware of the fact, were merely repeating what Prince Philip himself had been thinking and saying for some little time. Prince Philip's views on children's upbringing stem mainly from his own uninhibited and somewhat unorthodox education, and his public utterances have pointed the fact on numerous occasions.

"The art of education," he has said, "is to combine formal training with as wide a variety of experiences as possible *including some which involve a calculated risk*." (The italics are ours.) "I think education is intended to produce intelligent, morally strong, self-sufficient human beings willing and capable of improving the machinery of living which man has created for his enjoyment."

He has also given his own definition of education.

"The very term 'education' means different things to different people," he has said. "To some it means mere book-learning and the ability to pass examinations, some again concentrate on the powers of reasoning and observation, to others it means preparation for life and citizenship, but to most of us it means a bit of all these things. The difficulty is that while the purely book-learning side can be measured by standards and examinations, the development of character is highly individual and cannot be measured by classes or at stated intervals. Neither can the training of intellect and the development of character be done separately, because character will be formed whether it is guided into the right paths or whether it is neglected and no amount of intellectual training will make up for that neglect."

And perhaps he was thinking particularly of his own son on the occasion when he said, "Once a boy is aware of his own possibilities, his confidence increases and his sense of uncertainty in a rather bewildering world is correspondingly reduced."

Whether he was specifically thinking of Charles or not when he said that, he had no intention, as subsequent events have clearly shown, of permitting his son to grow up lacking confidence in a rather bewildering world, as might perhaps have been the case had nanny and governess been succeeded by private tutors.

Until now, Prince Charles had been largely brought up amidst the cosy and perhaps cloying atmosphere of the royal nursery and the nursery schoolroom. His father apart, he was surrounded on all sides by the petticoat influence of his nanny and governess, his mother and his sister. Prince Philip saw the danger clearly and set about the task of uprooting the boy and transplanting him to a more invigorating youthful environment, similar to that which he had experienced himself in childhood.

Prince Philip's own upbringing was considerably unorthodox by royal standards. He was only eighteen months old when his family was forced into exile from their native Greece. He never learned to speak the Greek language and cannot do so to this day.

The age of six found him attending an American kindergarten for the children of U.S. businessmen and diplomats in the Paris suburb of St. Cloud, where he learned to speak English with a slight American accent. He was taken to and from school initially either on foot or by car, but later cycled backwards and forwards on his own. He saved up and bought the bicycle himself. One day he was about to set off home in a heavy shower when a teacher noticed that he had no raincoat. Asked about it, Philip replied that he was "saving up to buy one".

Even in those early days at St. Cloud he showed considerable enthusiasm for sport, learning to box and swim as well as chant American football songs!

From Paris, when he outgrew the kindergarten stage, he was sent to England, where he became a boarder at Cheam School, at that time located in Surrey. His school fees were paid, in part at least, by his mother's brother, the 2nd Marquess of Milford Haven, whom Philip knew as Uncle George. At Cheam he continued to display considerable sporting prowess, clearing a record three feet ten and a half inches in the under-12 high jump and winning the school diving championship. He spent the Easter and Christmas vacations either with his maternal grandmother at Kensington Palace or with Uncle George and his family at Lynden Manor in Berkshire. During the long summer vacation, until his parents drifted apart and his sisters had all married German princes, he returned to his home in the Rue du Mont Valerien in Paris.

Coincidence shaped the next step in his education. Under the patronage of Prince Max of Baden, a remarkable and far-sighted man named Dr. Kurt Hahn had founded a remarkable and unorthodox school . . . Salem, where the basic principle of education was to train boys to leadership through teaching them to serve others.

Theodora, the last of Prince Philip's sisters to get married, had become the wife of Prince Max's son, Berthold, at that time headmaster of Salem. So it came about that Philip, on the fringe of his teenage years, transferred from Cheam to Salem, a school housed in a wing of a German *schloss* on the shores of Lake Constance, where he found himself living a hard and healthy life which involved swimming in strong currents, sailing small boats and scaling mountains in addition to more orthodox scholastic pursuits.

But he also found himself in an uneasy and fast-changing Germany where the Nazis were busy cementing their newly-won power. Kurt Hahn was arrested and it was fortunate for him that he had friends in high places outside Germany. Under pressure, the Nazis agreed to release him and permitted him to quit the country. Britain was perhaps an obvious choice for the exiled schoolmaster and the principles he had rooted originally at Salem were now transplanted to Gordonstoun in Scotland.

The youthful Philip was soon to follow him to Gordonstoun. Philip was then, as now, a high-spirited individual with a sharp and sometimes caustic sense of humour. He was not above making mock of the goose-stepping, jackbooted Nazis and things came to something of a head after he had poked fun at the Nazi salute, so reminiscent, to the schoolboy mind, of the raised hand seeking permission to leave the classroom.

"We thought it better, both for Philip and us, if he left Germany," one of his sisters was to explain later.

So Philip, after something less than a year at Salem, transferred to Gordonstoun, on the shores of the Moray Firth . . . and here he stayed until he went to the Royal Naval College at Dartmouth, working hard and playing hard, displaying quick intelligence, pride of workmanship, meticulous attention to detail along with schoolboy high spirits and a lively sense of fun.

He shone at mathematics, geography and modern languages. He represented Gordonstoun in the Scottish schools' athletic championships and captained the school at both cricket and hockey. He worked with his hands as well as with his head, helping to convert old stables into comfortable dormitories as the school grew and expanded. But the sea became his great passion. He spent nearly every free moment at nearby Hopeman Harbour, working on small boats, going on trips to the fishing grounds with the local fishermen. He helped to sail the school schooner round the west coast of Scotland and across the North Sea to Norway, working in the galley for part of the trip.

"Thoroughly trustworthy," wrote his seamanship instructor in one report, "and not afraid of dirty and arduous work." Dr. Hahn added that his qualities of leadership were most noticeable, "though marred at times by impatience and intolerance".

Such slight weaknesses did not prevent Philip from rising to the position of Guardian (head boy) before finally leaving Gordonstoun for Dartmouth and a career in the Royal Navy.

"Prince Philip," wrote Dr. Hahn in his final report, "is universally trusted, liked and respected. He has the greatest sense of service of all the boys in the school.

"Prince Philip is a born leader, but will need the exacting demands of a great service to do justice to himself. His best is outstanding; his second best is not good enough.

"Prince Philip will make his mark in any profession where he will have to prove himself in a full trial of strength."

It was perhaps no more than poetic justice that one of Prince Philip's early public engagements was to confer a degree on his old headmaster.

"The hero of Charles Kingsley's *Westward Ho!*" he recalled in his speech on that occasion, "was expelled for hitting his headmaster over the head with a slate."

He grinned broadly at Dr. Hahn and held out the velvet hat symbolising the degree he was about to confer upon him.

"I invite you, sir . . ."

And now, at the beginning of 1957, his own schooldays nearly twenty years behind him, Prince Philip could look ahead to the day when his son, Britain's future King, would follow in his footsteps at Gordonstoun. A pointer to what was in his mind was given, in the roundabout fashion in which such things so often become public, in a statement emanating from the British Information Service in Washington. This quoted Philip as saying concerning Prince Charles: "We want him to go to school with other boys of his generation and to learn to live with other children and to absorb from childhood the discipline imposed by education with others".

So, by small and subtle degrees, began the task of turning the future King from a child in the palace nursery to a schoolboy in the classroom. Dancing lessons ended; music lessons were, for a time at least, curtailed. Instead, three afternoons a week Charles went along to a Chelsea playing field to enjoy his first experience of schoolboy football, with small red flags to represent the goal-posts, and to trot round the running track with a number of other small boys. On two other afternoons each week an inconspicuous royal car took him unobtrusively to a private gymnasium in a Cheslea mews where he pulled himself up the climbing bars, swung along the parallel bars and underwent a course of similar physical exercises in company with fourteen other youngsters.

The task the Queen and Prince Philip had set themselves in attempting to give their small son the broadest, most varied, most down-to-earth education of any prince in history was no easy one. The difficulties which lay ahead were immediately apparent following his very first visit to that Chelsea gymnasium, as excited parents of the other small boys busily telephoned each other with news of what little Tom, Dick or Harry had had to say about the new companion who was their future King.

III

At half-past nine one damp January morning the royal

experiment which was to lead, in time, to Cheam, Gordonstoun and Timbertop took its next tentative step forward. An inconspicuous black saloon car, nicknamed 'Mighty One' by Buckingham Palace servants on account of its registration number —MYT 1—drew up in front of a five-storey, brick-built Victorian house in Hans Place, Knightsbridge. Out of the car stepped a small boy in a velvet-collared coat which effectively disguised the fact that underneath he was wearing a cinnamon-coloured blazer with H.H. woven in gold on the breast pocket. For the first time in England's long history, the heir to the Throne—at a cost of £30 a term—was taking his place among other boys in an ordinary schoolroom.

The school was Hill House, and its choice, in part at least, was almost certainly dictated by its location, a convenient short car ride from Buckingham Palace. It was so near, indeed, that after he had been there only a short time Charles asked his mother if he couldn't walk to school, as some of the other boys did, instead of going by car. The idea, though it displayed the right schoolboy spirit, was promptly and gently discounted. For a start, walking to school would have involved crossing several busy intersections and the eight-year-old Prince was hardly accustomed to going about the streets of London. More important perhaps, the sight of the heir to the Throne actually walking to and from school would have aroused that very degree of public interest his parents were most anxious to avoid.

Despite the unobtrusiveness with which the operation was carried out, there was, that first day, a considerable gathering of photographers, reporters and eager-beaver sightseers around the school entrance as the royal car drew up and Miss Peebles accompanied her small charge into the school building. Perhaps that was only to be expected. But when a yet larger crowd was reported at the beginning of school hours on the third day of the experiment, the Queen felt it was time to take a firm stand in the matter of her son's upbringing.

She declined to let him leave Buckingham Palace that day until word reached her that the crowd of would-be sightseers had largely given up hope of seeing the young Prince and had begun to disperse. Only then did she allow Charles to leave for school, where he arrived forty-five minutes late. And later that day, the palace press officer was busily telephoning the editors of national newspapers with a royal request that they should withdraw their photographers and give the Queen's son a fair chance of going to school like any ordinary boy.

For Prince Charles, it was a gentle enough introduction to schoolboy life, a soft-centre transitional period between the cosy isolation of the palace schoolroom and the hurly-burly of boarding school life. Except for the headmaster, Col. Henry Townend, an Oxford blue and former England athlete, who taught the boys geography, Latin and French as well as instructing them in the rudiments of football, and, in photographs at least, looked not unlike Prince Philip, the teachers at Hill House were all female, including the headmaster's wife, who taught anatomy and general knowledge. School began at half-past nine each morning with prayers and the singing of the school hymn. Lessons included reading and writing, arithmetic, history and geography, elementary science, botany and anatomy. There were also classes in painting, modelling, singing and acting. A mid-morning break for milk was followed by light exercise in the school's pint-sized gymnasium with its punch-ball, rope ladders and basket ball, and its windows protected by wire mesh against the occasionally unruly exuberance of small boys letting off steam. More lessons followed until lunch-time, after which there was a two-mile trek to the playing field for football or cricket with eight-a-side softball in the gymnasium as an alternative if it was wet.

Undeniably nervous at first, as most small boys are on their first day at school, Charles settled in very quickly among the 102 other boys at Hill House, the sons of doctors and barristers, diplomats and civil servants, actors and journalists, their ages ranging from five to ten. That first day in the classroom he painted a schoolboyish watercolour of a green ship making its way under London Bridge against a background of blue sky, signing it 'Charles' in pencil, and everyone seemed mildly surprised that he should have gobbled up his lunch—stewed meat with boiled potatoes and carrots followed by rhubarb and apple tart—like any other healthy youngster.

For a number of reasons, the experiment never fully succeeded.

It was all too much of an exciting novelty for loyal Londoners. Though the crowds outside the school diminished, there was seldom a morning when there was not at least a small handful of people eager to see Charles arrive. Miss Peebles, after that first morning, no longer accompanied him to school, though there was always a royal detective to keep a watchful eye on his comings and goings. Even his unscheduled departures for the school playing field, walking in a long crocodile of small boys, politely raising his school cap to car drivers who pulled up to give the boys right of way at pedestrian crossings, were usually witnessed by a small ring of watchful eyes and some of his early efforts at booting a football and swinging a cricket bat were executed under the unseen gaze of a distant telephoto lens.

In addition, exposure to schoolboy life also exposed the young Prince to schoolboy ailments. Six days after he first enrolled he was taken ill with tonsilitis and this kept him away from school for the next three weeks. He succumbed to a further attack of tonsilitis some four months later and this time it was deemed wise to exorcise the offending tonsils. This comparatively minor job of surgery was carried out in the Buhl Room suite at Buckingham Palace, where Charles had been born, though later, when it became Anne's turn to undergo a tonsillectomy, the Queen decided that for the future her children should go into hospital on such occasions so that all the aids of modern medicine might be immediately available in case of emergency.

As he lay in bed following the operation, Prince Charles talked with Jack Vernon, an operating theatre attendant from the Great Ormond Street Hospital for Sick Children who was at the palace to clear away the surgical equipment. Among other things, Mr. Vernon mentioned that he had a young daughter named Maureen who was only a month older than Prince Charles.

Charles asked if Maureen would like him to write to her.

"I'm sure she would," said Mr. Vernon.

The young Prince produced an official Buckingham Palace card embossed with the royal crest, wrote on it, "To Maureen, Love from Charles" and gave it to the delighted Mr. Vernon to take home to his daughter.

According to a former royal servant, Prince Charles wanted to know what his tonsils looked like and they were given to him, suitably preserved, in a small container. He kept them among his books and toys in the nursery for some considerable time afterwards, displaying them with boyish pride to members of the palace staff and to school friends he brought home with him for tea from time to time.

Surgery was followed by a period of convalescence at Holkham Hall, the home of the Earl and Countess of Leicester, a few miles from the Queen's own home at Sandringham on Norfolk's dry, bracing and sometimes windy coast, where he played on the sandy beach and displayed keen interest in the small potter's shop his hostess had recently established on the Holkham estate. The potters responded to his obvious enthusiasm by showing him some of the tricks of the trade and when he returned to Buckingham Palace it was as the proud possessor of a piggy bank he had helped to fashion himself.

IV

Anne, who always wanted to do everything her big brother did, wanted badly to go to school with him. Of course, she couldn't. To prevent her feeling too lonely in the absence of her brother, the Queen arranged for two other small girls, Susan Babington-Smith, the daughter of a banker, and Caroline Hamilton, daughter of a company director, to visit the palace daily and share her lessons with her.

Lessons started each day at half-past nine and continued until fifteen minutes to one, with a brief break each morning for orange squash and biscuits. Except on Tuesday, the other two girls would take their leave at lunchtime. Tuesday was Brownie day, when the palace Brownie pack, to which Anne and her two friends belonged, held its weekly meeting in the large, lofty Centre Room overlooking the Victoria Monument. During the warmer weather of the summer months these meetings were transferred to the octagonal-shaped summer-house in the gardens.

Like Charles, Anne studied the piano under Miss Hilda Bor and had French lessons from a visiting tutor. On Wednesdays, in company with five other small girls, the daughters of friends and acquaintances of the Royal Family, she took part in the dancing class which was held in the Music Room overlooking the palace gardens.

With Prince Charles now at school and Princess Anne spending most of each day at her lessons, there was no longer necessity for such a large staff in the royal nursery and Mrs. Lightbody, the children's nanny, took her leave of Buckingham Palace. The two children were both extremely attached to Mrs. Lightbody and Charles, in particular, was reportedly quite upset at her leaving. But 'Mamba' (Mabel Anderson) stayed on to supervise the running of the nursery, a fact which was to prove fortunate in the light of future events.

Whatever childlike regret Prince Charles may have felt over the departure of Mrs. Lightbody was quickly counteracted by the novelty of his new life as a schoolboy at Hill House. With the school's annual field day not far off, he was soon enthusiastically engaged in preparations for a special event he had suggested. Some of the Hill House boys were to give their own version of the naval gun-carriage race which forms so exciting a part of the Royal Tournament each year. To this end, a mock field-gun with wheels three feet in diameter and a barrel measuring some seven feet was constructed in the school workshop, and when field day came round the Queen and Prince Philip were among the parents who watched Charles and six other small boys manhandle it across a make-believe chasm. They also saw their small son demonstrate his new-found ability at cricket and come fourth out of nine competitors in the 50-yard dash.

There was a brief hitch in the proceedings involving the imitation field-gun when part of the weapon thudded to the ground while being manhandled into position.

"That would have gone into the water if there'd been any water," commented one of the schoolboy gun crew.

Notwithstanding this mishap, the operation was completed in some seven minutes as against the full half-hour it had taken during rehearsal and it was a proud Prince Charles who lined up his small crew at the end of the proceedings and presented them to his parents.

"Well done," his father complimented them, briskly.

8   *Off to School*

For youngsters, the end of the holidays is perhaps never a particularly happy time, signifying, as it does, a loss of freedom and a return to the classroom. For Prince Charles, the end of his customary stay at Balmoral in the summer of 1957 was perhaps approached with more glumness than usual. He was not yet nine and, following two terms as a day boy at Hill House, going backwards and forwards to school from his home at Buckingham Palace, he was going now to his first boarding school. The school selected for this next and important stage of educating the future King was Cheam, the preparatory school his father had attended before him, though since Prince Philip's day it had moved its location from Surrey to the borders of Berkshire and Hampshire, some fifty-six miles from London.

At Hill House he had been making steady, if unspectacular, progress. But his French, in particular, was not progressing as the Queen would have wished. To help improve it, his mother engaged a young French-speaking companion, Mlle. Bibiane de Roujoux, to stay with the royal children at Balmoral that summer. Mlle. de Roujoux, recommended to the Royal Family by Mme. Untermeyer, who taught the Queen her own fluent French in childhood, lived with the children in the nursery, went out and about with them, had her meals with the Royal Family.

"We speak nothing but French at meal-times," the Queen told one visitor to Balmoral around this time, adding by way of explanation, "It's to help Charles."

Such meal-time conversations proved of benefit. The young Prince's school report at the end of his first year at Cheam included marks of fifty-two per cent. for French and later, when his mother paid one of her rare visits to the school and presented the prizes, she had the added pleasure of handing one to her own son for 'improved proficiency' in this particular subject.

In sending their son to boarding school, the Queen and Prince Philip were perhaps only following in the tradition of Britain's upper classes. But they were, at the same time, making a distinct and striking departure from the old royal tradition of education by governess and tutor. It was not perhaps so big a break with tradition as some people would have had them make. Yet, on the whole, the choice of Cheam as an educational establishment for the future King represented a happy compromise between time-honoured tradition and the views of a rather vociferous minority that the boy should be educated at a more ordinary school.

The royal decision to send Prince Charles to Cheam had not been arrived at without considerable thought, and, on his mother's side at least, perhaps not without some slight initial misgivings. Before making her decision, the Queen had also visited other possible educational establishments, looking around the school buildings and talking with the headmasters, and it was perhaps something more than a coincidence that a number of prominent educationists were among the guests invited to informal luncheon parties at Buckingham Palace around this time.

But in the end, it was presumably her husband's advice which weighed with her most and his old school which won the day.

Apart from the fact that Prince Philip had been educated at Cheam before going to Salem and Gordonstoun, there were several other factors in its favour. It was reasonably near London. It was reasonably secluded, standing in its own sixty-five acres of well-wooded grounds. It had that indefinable something known as 'background', having been about the task of educating upper-crust Britons, at various locations, since somewhere around the middle of the seventeenth century, though it was not at this particular time an especially fashionable school. Above all, it was a school which aimed at producing an all-round boy rather than a scholarship specialist and this was how the Queen and her husband visualised the future King . . . an all-round man, as, indeed, Prince Philip himself undoubtedly is. School fees may not have counted with the Queen, though it is interesting to note that the fees at

Cheam, increased from £94 10s. to £100 a term around this time, were about average or a little less than average for a school of its type.

Charles, in company with his parents and Princess Anne, had visited the school before the final choice was irrevocably made. He saw the classrooms with their ancient desks carved and scratched by successive generations of schoolboys and the dormitories with their Spartan-like beds of flock mattresses mounted on wooden planks.

The Queen, herself, tested one of the beds by sitting on it. "Well, you won't be able to bounce on that," she told her son, with a smile.

Prince Philip, in fatherly fashion, assured his small son that his own years at Cheam had been among the happiest days of his life.

All of which did little to reassure the young Prince during the long, overnight train journey from Balmoral to London at the start of his schooldays. Usually a hearty young trencherman, he was noticeably content to do little more than toy with his meals during the journey.

His parents drove to Cheam with him, handed him over to the care of the school authorities, said their goodbyes and left him with his large leather trunk with its brass nameplate labelled Prince Charles and a consoling box of milk chocolates and chocolate biscuits.

One of the royal detectives, Reginald Summers, was detailed to keep a watchful eye on things. Initially, the detective lived in a cottage in the school grounds. His on-the-spot presence at that time was considered essential. Even this out-of-the-way spot in wooded countryside attracted the inevitable sightseers and tele-photo lenses once the young Prince was in residence at Cheam. Buckingham Palace raised the question of the telephoto lenses with newspaper editors and the school's joint headmasters issued an appeal to the general public to be left alone "to get on with the job of educating ninety small boys, which is a fairly full-time occupation".

Things improved after that and later it was necessary for the royal detective to visit Cheam only at weekends, watching over the future King whenever he travelled by bus for soccer games with other schools and when he left the school grounds on Sunday mornings with the other boys to attend morning service at the local church.

Inevitably, his first few days at Cheam found the young Prince somewhat out of his element. Not counting weekends at Windsor, holidays at Balmoral and Sandringham, which were, after all, simply secondary homes to him, it was the first time he had been away from the vast palace he called his home. It was the first time he had found himself living, eating and sleeping with strangers, even though the strangers were boys of his own age.

The first encounter with boarding school is a considerable shock for any small boy, and the shock must have been doubly so for a boy accustomed to the cosy confines of the royal nursery. Instead of going to bed in his own private room, he now found himself sharing a dormitory with nine other boys. The dormitory itself was vastly different from the comfortable surroundings he had become accustomed to in the palace nursery. The floor lacked carpet and the room was unheated, though in winter the windows were closed during the day and the dormitory door left open for warm air rising from downstairs to raise the temperature a degree or two. But at bedtimes the windows had to be opened again, however cold the night. His bed, too, lacked the comfort of the one he had left behind in the palace nursery, consisting of a flock mattress perched upon the wooden slats of a battered, century-old bed. He had always been brought up to do a good deal for himself, but now he had to do much more. He had to clean his own shoes, make his own bed each morning, fold and tidy his own clothes when it was time for bed at night.

For the young Prince, this first experience of boarding school life must have been a strange and perhaps sometimes frightening experience, even if cartoonists and comedians found it a subject for jest. When the Queen and Prince Philip attended the Royal Variety Show that year, those zany comics known as the Crazy Gang, never backward in pulling royal legs, appeared on stage dressed as somewhat overgrown schoolboys complaining loudly about the hardness of their beds. Point was added to the joke by the production of three wooden planks which ended up in the orchestra pit.

The royal parents were reported to have thought the skit highly amusing. "I could hardly stop laughing," the Queen is said to have commented after the show.

Her small son, on the other hand, found little to laugh about during his first few weeks at boarding school. As other less regal small boys have discovered before and since, the monastic, almost exclusively male atmosphere of a boys' boarding school comes as a not inconsiderable ordeal to youngsters experiencing it for the first time. After the quietness and seclusion of life in the royal nursery, it was perhaps understandable if Prince Charles at first found life among a noisy mass of some ninety other youngsters more than a trifle overwhelming. It was perhaps equally understandable if a natural sense of awe among the other boys caused an initial tendency to avoid his company, a state of affairs which his own inherited shyness did little to counteract.

Until he went to Cheam, it is doubtful if Prince Charles had ever in his life heard a voice raised in anger or seen a blow struck in temper. There may have been the occasional reprimand from his mother or nanny, the still more occasional spanking from his father, the occasional push or pinch from his small sister, but nothing more. Now all around him were lusty young males who seemed to delight in jeers and jibes, shouting, punching and wrestling furiously upon the least provocation, and sometimes with no apparent provocation at all. The schoolboy skylarking which went on in the wash-room or in the dormitory after lights out must have come as a further ordeal for the young Prince, as indeed for other small boys joining the school at the same time. And Cheam being no different from any other boys' boarding school, there must inevitably have been also some degree of bullying from which the royal 'new bug' cannot altogether have escaped. But if he was ever bullied, as surely he was, then he was also boy enough to appeal to neither his parents nor the school authorities for help.

For their part, the school authorities were careful not to make his existing specialness as the future King any more special through any show of untoward interference on their part. This, they knew, was the very last thing either the Queen or Prince Philip would have desired.

In sending her son to Cheam, the Queen's instructions to the school's joint headmasters, Mark Wheeler and Peter Beck, had been explicit. They boiled down to this: Treat my son just as you would any other boy.

On the Queen's suggestion, the two headmasters, in advance of Prince Charles' arrival at the school, sent a letter to the parents of their other pupils.

"It is the wish of the Queen and Prince Philip," they wrote, "that there shall be no alteration in the way the school is run and that Prince Charles shall be treated the same as the other boys.

"The staff will call and refer to him as Prince Charles, but the boys will call him Charles. It would be a great help if you could explain this to your boys.

"His parents' wishes are that he should be given exactly the same education and upbringing as the other boys in the school."

So the boy destined to be King found himself standing in line twice a week for the privilege of taking a hot bath and having his hands and neck checked for cleanliness by the school matron, Stella Jack, an imposing and immaculate figure in her blue uniform with the starched cuffs, before he was permitted to sit down for breakfast each morning.

Schooldays began promptly at fifteen minutes past seven each morning when the master on duty popped his head round the door of the dormitory and gave a brisk call of "Rise and shine."

The time factor represented no special hardship. As long as he could remember, Charles had always been up and about not later than half-past seven in the morning. Neither the Queen nor Prince Philip have ever encouraged their children to lie abed late, even on holidays.

Face and hands washed, his teeth cleaned, dressed in his school uniform with its grey jacket and short trousers, Prince Charles duly presented himself for matron's inspection and attended prayers in the school hall. There was also a brief morning ceremony of shaking hands with the headmasters, a custom he shared with all the other boys.

There was, from the outset, never any question of royal privilege or segregation. He was, as his parents desired, treated like any other boy at the school. He ate his meals with the rest of the school, sitting on one of the long benches arrayed round the bare wooden tables in the panelled dining hall under the glassy gaze of the stuffed stag's head mounted above the main door. From time to time, he took his turn in waiting upon the other boys at his table.

Breakfast consisted usually of porridge or cereal, followed by bacon and egg or steamed fish, with bread and butter and marmalade to fill any empty schoolboy corners that yet remained. Lessons in a green-walled classroom started at nine o'clock, with three forty-minute periods leading up to a mid-morning break when there was a bun to eat and a glass of milk. Two more periods of lessons—history or geography, mathematics, French or Latin (a comparatively new addition to the school's basic curriculum)—followed before one o'clock lunch.

For lunch, there was a main course of meat or sometimes fish, followed by dessert—rice or semolina, lemon tart or suet pudding. There is a story that the first time he found himself served with chocolate-flavoured semolina, Prince Charles was seen to be toying with it with little sign of enthusiasm.

One of the masters is said to have asked him if he didn't like it.

"Not very much, sir," the young Prince replied. Then, as though feeling that some additional explanation was needed, he reportedly added the small, but revealing, item of information that "We don't often have sweet desserts at home."

He was understandably puzzled by a dessert called 'stodge' the first time he encountered it.

"Stodge?" he queried. "I've never heard of it. What is it? Is it English?"

It was, he found, very English. 'Stodge' is Cheam's schoolboy slang for rice pudding.

Lunch each day was followed by a brief compulsory period—known for fairly obvious reasons as 'Digest'—when the boys went to their dormitories to rest before resuming work. Two afternoons in each week—Wednesdays and Saturdays—were devoted to sport, soccer and rugby football in winter, cricket and swimming in summer, under the watchful eye and expert coaching of Jack Mauldren, the grey-haired sports master who had taught Prince Philip something of the manly art of self-defence during his years at Cheam.

Other afternoon activities included art and handicrafts, both of which the young Prince thoroughly enjoyed and for which he revealed considerable youthful talent. 'High tea' at six o'clock consisted of such schoolboy delicacies as baked beans, sardines on toast, scrambled or boiled eggs, followed by bread and butter with jam or honey.

Bed for Prince Charles and other small boys of the same age was at seven o'clock.

Saturday evening, when there was a film show in the dining hall, brought a welcome change from ordinary school routine. The films consisted mostly of westerns and slapstick comedies. Extremely popular with Charles, as with many of the other boys because of audience identity with what was taking place on the screen, were the antics of boys and masters in the old Will Hay comedies of schoolboy life.

On Sunday mornings Charles walked in orderly file with the other boys through the school grounds and along the main road to the village church of St. Peter's in the neighbouring village of Headley. On Sunday afternoon he would sit down to write his weekly 'duty' letter to his parents at Buckingham Palace in conformity with the Cheam tradition.

The story that he was embarrassed in church by the inclusion of prayers for himself and others of the Royal Family and expressed the wish that they "would pray for the other chaps, too" is probably apocryphal. But the pew in which he sat now bears the inscription, 'Prince Charles Sat Here', carved into the ancient woodwork by some wag with a penknife.

II

Gradually, his initial nervousness thawed out and the young Prince merged imperceptibly into schoolboy life, even to the extent of having a pin-up picture hidden inside the door of his locker. It was an innocent enough schoolboy pin-up—his pet corgi, Whisky.

By the time his ninth birthday came round he had begun to feel his schoolboy feet. Among those he invited to his birthday party was the school's head boy.

"That's rather an honour for you," one of the young Prince's new-found school friends remarked when he heard that the head boy, a remote and lofty personage in schoolboy minds, had accepted the invitation.

"It's rather an honour for him, too," Prince Charles is said to have replied.

It is a fact that throughout his years at Cheam he displayed a certain natural and ingrained regal reserve which would not permit him to join in the shouting and name-calling in which many of his schoolfellows indulged so freely. Yet he proved early on that he was no namby-pamby and well able to hold his own in schoolboy scuffles.

There was an occasion in the wash-room when another boy, somewhat older and certainly bigger, thought it a great lark to seize hold of his future King and duck his head under the stream of cold water gushing from one of the taps. It was a highly indignant Prince Charles who broke free of his assailant and went on to learn one of those lessons of schoolboy life which are not included in any school curriculum but are perhaps more important than any academic subject.

His teacher, on this occasion, was the school barber who was in the wash-room at the time and witnessed the incident.

"You're not going to stand for that, are you?" he said to Charles. "I know I wouldn't."

Neither did the young Prince. He promptly proceeded to tackle the bigger boy with such vigour that he succeeded in tipping him into a bath full of water . . . and such was the impetus of his school-boy retaliation that he fell in on top of his adversary.

There were, during those early days at Cheam, several other occasions when the young Prince was seen struggling or wrestling with other small boys. Sometimes such tussles were the outcome of sheer schoolboy high spirits; occasionally they were the climax of some boyish disagreement.

Inevitably, royal youngsters being no different from any other youngsters, the Queen's son was involved in the occasional schoolboy prank. There seems no reason to doubt the story that a master at Cheam was walking along one of the school corridors one day when he was almost bowled over by two small boys who shot out of a cloakroom, struggling to free themselves of coats draped over their heads which effectively prevented them from seeing where they were going.

Investigation inside the cloakroom revealed Prince Charles and another small boy perched in ambush on the water pipes, a vantage point from which they were dropping raincoats over the heads of any other youngsters who came in before leaping down on them and bundling them back into the corridor.

As time progressed, Charles made several friends, though, for him, schoolboy friendships came neither quickly nor easily. With his friends, he doubtless visited the school kitchen to ask the cook for the mutton bones, five to a set, needed for Cheam's traditional game of 'jacks', which involved sitting cross-legged on the floor, tossing the bones into the air and catching them on the back of the hand.

His royal parents played their part in ensuring that he was neither spoiled nor accorded any special schoolboy privileges on account of his birth, background or future position. Each term after the first he journeyed back to Cheam at the beginning of each fresh term not in one of the royal cars, but by train, travelling second class with a party of his schoolfellows. At Newbury station, five miles from the school, he would stand in line with the rest of the boys, waiting his turn to board the school bus.

It was something of a tradition at Cheam, Charles found, for the boys to each have a model yacht which they raced against one another on the school pond. It is not unreasonable to assume that one of his early letters sent home to his parents at Buckingham Palace included a boyish plea for a yacht of his own so that he could join in. Certainly, in due course, he received one. But it was not the tall, glossy, super-magnificent craft of which schoolboy dreams are made and which his royal parents might so easily have sent him. On the contrary, it proved to be among the smallest of the model craft in his dormitory.

He received the same amount of pocket-money as any other junior at Cheam—twenty-five shillings a term. As with all other small boys, there were doubtless times when funds ran out and he reportedly sold such cherished boyhood treasures as marbles and a pocket-knife to raise cash for visits to the school tuckshop. In America, this news came to the notice of the Retail Candy Stores Institute, which, with typical American generosity (and perhaps an eye to publicity), promptly shipped some fifty pounds of assorted candy, chocolates, chewing gum, jelly beans and peanut butter to Britain to make royal schooldays more pleasurable.

Inevitably, and almost imperceptibly, the young Prince was beginning to change. He was, of course, growing all the time. He was also shedding much of his puppy fat. Football, cricket and swimming were making him leaner and more muscular. There was more colour in his cheeks. He had, from babyhood, always been a good eater. But now, if anything, he ate more heartily than ever, and if there was one meal-time when he was reproved by the supervising master for shovelling stew on to his fork with a piece of bread in rather un-princely fashion, then the incident is surely understandable in the light of schoolboy appetites.

But the change being wrought in him was more than merely physical. He was, according to someone who had the opportunity of seeing him from time to time around this stage of his life, changing also in other, more subtle, ways. He was losing something of his earlier pensive seriousness, becoming somewhat less shy and nervous in human relationships. He frowned less; smiled and laughed more.

The change in him was perhaps illustrated by a small, schoolboy incident which followed the gift of a new cricket bat in the summer term. Unlike his parents' parting gift of chocolates when he first went to Cheam, which he had kept to himself because he was too shy to offer them to anyone else, he now wanted all his new school-boy friends to try out the new cricket bat.

But one boy clung to the bat rather too long for the Prince's spirit of fairness.

"What do you think you're doing—practising for a Test Match?" Charles reportedly remarked as he took the bat from him and passed it over to the boy whose turn it was next.

He enjoyed sports, though, swimming apart, he did not revel in them to quite the same passionate degree his father had displayed in schooldays. At swimming he excelled. His father, in his younger days, was said to 'swim like a fish and dive like a seal'. Charles displayed much the same aquatic ability.

At football, by his second winter at Cheam, he proved suffi-ciently good to earn a place in the school Colts, turning out in white shorts, a red shirt and red-striped grey socks for games against rival schools such as Horris Hill and St. George's, Windsor.

At home, Charles had long been encouraged to join in conversa-tion, both with his family and visitors, and this fact was to prove useful following one football game when the boys of both teams paired off for tea in the Cheam tradition. Charles found himself responsible for entertaining a somewhat dour youngster who stared stolidly ahead of him, perhaps out of sheer nervousness at finding himself sitting with his future King, and tucked into his food with hardly a word.

It was left to Prince Charles to carry on what was at first a some-what one-sided conversation, leading and steering it in a not unskilful attempt at bringing the other boy out of his shell. So successful was he that by the end of the meal the two of them were observed to be laughing and joking together as though they had been friends for years.

At this stage of his schoolboy career, art and handicrafts enthused the young Prince perhaps more than sports and games. Some of his happiest days at Cheam were those spent in the school workshop, where he proved extremely adept with his hands. The end of each term saw him returning home to Buckingham Palace with something new he had made. The Royal Family and members of the nursery staff were alike recipients of what he brought.

He made a small wooden table as a birthday present for his small sister, Princess Anne. He made a pen-stand for Miss Peebles, a tea-tray for Miss Anderson. For his mother he fashioned a small book-rack which was still in use in quite recent times in the Queen's sitting room at Windsor Castle. Later, when his baby brother, Prince Andrew, was born, he made him a rocking elephant.

Academically, he proved himself a fairly average scholar, bright in some subjects, a trifle behindhand in others. The end of his first year at Cheam found him top of a class of some twenty boys in geography. The world globe and wall atlas in the palace school-room had given him a good grounding, enabling him to gain seventy marks out of a possible hundred. His French was improving. He gained fifty-two marks out of a hundred and the highest mark in class was no more than sixty-five. He was good at art, weak at mathematics. The story that one history lesson revealed a somewhat surprising gap in his knowledge is perhaps apocryphal, but it will doubtless pass into legend that King Charles III, during his early school days, knew nothing of the abdication of the king who became Duke of Windsor and thus changed the course of royal history.

9   *Prince of Wales*

I

It was the final day of the Empire and Common wealth Games, being held that year of 1958 in Cardiff, the capital of Wales. On and off, the Queen had not been in the best of health for some little time past. She had been plagued with successive colds and chills since returning from her royal tour of Canada and the United States the previous October. But obstinately dutiful in matters of royal moment, as always, she had continued to carry out her traditional functions, even to the extent of riding on horseback in the pouring rain for the annual ceremony of Trooping the Colour on her official birthday. She had followed that with a tour of Scotland and North-East England, but this she had been forced to cut short, leaving Prince Philip to carry through on his own while she returned to Buckingham Palace with another severe cold. A subsequent operation relieved her long-standing catarrhal sinusitis.

To the disappointment of the Welsh people, she was compelled, on the firm advice of her physicians, to abandon a projected tour of Wales and her attendance at the closing ceremonies of the Empire and Commonwealth Games. Welsh disappointment was partly assuaged, however, by the news that Prince Philip would attend on his own.

But the Queen, with her excellent sense of timing and the fitness of things, also had a surprise in store.

As soon as she was sufficiently recovered from her operation, with the connivance of the British Broadcasting Corporation and the help of a B.B.C. engineer, she recorded her own personal message for the people of Wales. The recording completed to her satisfaction, it was carefully packed and consigned secretly to Cardiff, where Prince Philip awaited it.

Apart from the Queen, Prince Philip and the recording engineer, few people had any inkling of the dramatic contents of that recording. But one small boy was privy to the royal secret. At Cheam School, Prince Charles, still a month or so short of his tenth birthday, hugged his secret to himself as he and a handful of close friends made their way to the headmaster's sitting room to hear the recording broadcast from Cardiff.

His mother's voice, back to normal again after her long period of ill-health, came over clearly.

"By a cruel stroke of fate," she said, "I have been prevented from visiting North and South Wales and seeing something of the British Empire and Commonwealth Games. I regret particularly not being with you in Cardiff today for the closing ceremonies of this great meeting of Commonwealth athletes."

In the headmaster's sitting room at Cheam, the young Duke of Cornwall, as Charles still was, bounced up and down in his seat with suppressed excitement as his mother came to the real point of the recording and all the secrecy which had surrounded it.

"The British Empire and Commonwealth Games in the capital, together with all the activities of the Festival of Wales, have made this a memorable year for the Principality.

"I have therefore decided to mark it further by an act which will, I hope, give as much pleasure to all Welshmen as it does to me.

"I intend to create my son, Charles, Prince of Wales today."

So unexpected was the announcement that for a second there was complete silence among the 36,000 fervent Welsh people who packed the stadium at Cardiff that day. Then, as the impact of the Queen's announcement sank home, there was such an outburst of shouting and cheering that the royal recording had to be switched off momentarily while the tumult died down. Hats flew in the air, many to be lost for ever to their owners, women burst into tears, and sections of the crowd broke into song after the Welsh fashion. The song, of course, was *God Bless the Prince of Wales*.

When the uproar had partly died down, the Queen's voice was heard resuming her recorded speech:

"When he is grown up I will present him to you at Caernarvon."

II

Prince Charles was not yet ten on that historic day when his mother, by a recording, created him, in his absence, Prince of Wales. His immediate predecessor in that role, the Duke of Windsor, was created Prince of Wales on his sixteenth birthday, though it was just over a year later, on a swelteringly hot day in July, 1911, when he was ceremoniously invested with his princely coronet, along with the gold verge-staff and gold ring, and uttered a few words in Welsh taught him by the fiery Lloyd George . . . Heb Dduw, Heb ddim, Duw a digon—Without God, without anything, God is enough.

It was the revival of an ancient ceremony which had lapsed for centuries, and one over which the young Duke of Windsor was at first inclined to rebel. He objected strongly to the idea of dressing up in white satin knee-breeches and an ermine-trimmed surcoat of purple velvet. He was especially worried as to what his teenage friends would think of him in such an outlandish get-up.

His mother, the regal Queen Mary, did her best to resolve his concern.

"Your friends will understand," she said, "that as a prince you are obliged to do certain things which may seem a little silly."

The title of Prince of Wales goes back far into history. The story is that Edward I, to soothe the rebellious Welsh, appeared on the walls of Caernarvon Castle one April day in 1284, his infant son in his arms, and announced: "I give you a Prince of Wales, born in your own country and one who cannot speak a word of English."

How much of the story is fact and how much is legend it is difficult to resolve all these centuries later. The records show that Edward, the son, was not actually created Prince of Wales until 1301, but that does not entirely rule out the earlier story.

Contrary to popular belief, the eldest son of the Sovereign does not automatically become the Prince of Wales. The title is one that has to be conferred and can be withheld. Edward VII received the title when he was only a month old and held it until he became King nearly sixty years later. In consequence of this, George V was thirty-six before he, in turn, was created Prince of Wales. He, in turn, conferred the title on his eldest son shortly after he succeeded to the Throne.

When the Duke of Windsor ascended the Throne in 1936, and quickly abdicated, there was no Prince of Wales ... until now. Welshmen felt the omission keenly—so keenly that in 1943 Pwllheli Town Council asked the Prime Minister to recommend that King George VI should make his eldest daughter, the then Princess Elizabeth, Princess of Wales. It was pointed out, however, that the title was one traditionally reserved for the heir-apparent and could not, therefore, be conferred upon a girl.

In 1952, shortly after her accession to the Throne, Caernarvon petitioned the Queen to make Charles Prince of Wales. But the Queen felt that the boy was not then old enough and the time not yet ripe.

Now, at last, in 1958, the Welsh people could rejoice that they again had a Prince of their own.

III

The Queen had not yet fully recovered from the after-effects of her operation when Charles came to the end of his first year at Cheam and it was his small sister, Princess Anne, who drove there to meet him in the black estate car which went to collect him for the holiday. Charles had been to the village church of St. Peter's that morning with the rest of his schoolfellows, and Anne's arrival after lunch found him and a friend idling time away, tossing a ball from one to the other in the school drive, while their trunks and boxes stood packed and awaiting collection in the school hall.

There was, at this stage, the beginning of a new relationship developing between Charles and his young sister. Anne had always tended to copy everything her brother did, though in a spirit of tomboyish equality rather than small sister subservience. Indeed, her more extrovert nature had frequently found her dominating their brother-sister companionship. It was Anne who instigated many of their childhood adventures and she was, in addition, not above teasing her big brother when opportunity served. But now

116

it was Charles who began to dominate their youthful relationship, exerting a new-found masculine superiority which had already begun to emerge during that first year at Cheam. To Anne, eight years old that August, her brother, now that he was away at boarding school, came home on holiday as a personality commanding considerable admiration and respect.

That summer, following their usual practice, the two royal youngsters spent a few days with the Queen Mother at Sandringham House in Norfolk before travelling north to Scotland for the long summer stay at Balmoral.

'Going to stay with Granny' was, at this period of their lives, regarded as a considerable treat by both Charles and Anne.

At this age, they knew that 'Granny' could always be relied upon to ensure that their favourite dishes were served at meal-times . . . chicken for lunch with ice-cream to follow and eggs, either scrambled or lightly boiled, for afternoon tea. At Royal Lodge, Windsor, where they went to have tea with her sometimes on Sunday afternoons, there were always large boxes of chocolate and candy to hand into which they could dip. On holiday, they knew they could always persuade her to let them stay up just that little bit later at night and when their nanny came through from the nursery to announce that it was bedtime they would give the Queen Mother looks of childish pleading which she never could resist.

"Another ten minutes, Nanny," she would say, to their great delight.

There were, additionally, exciting shopping expeditions with her at holiday times and, not uncommonly, a little extra spending money.

There was one occasion, during the royal summer stay at Balmoral, when the Queen Mother took the two children shopping with her in nearby Ballater. She bought a doll for Anne and a toy crane for Charles. But Charles, always generous-hearted, wanted her to have something as well.

He caught her by the hand and tugged her towards the doorway of a small jewellery store.

"Come on, Granny," he cried, to the amusement of passers-by. "Now you must buy something for you, too."

The Queen Mother was once asked if she was not perhaps inclined to spoil her grandchildren.

"But of course," she replied. "Spoiling your grandchildren is half the fun of being a grandmother."

Where her grandchildren were concerned, nothing was—or is now, for that matter—too much trouble for her. Gifted with infinite patience and the ability to get down to the level of child-hood without any sense of condescension, she loved having them around her . . . and they loved being with her. At this stage of their lives, she played games such as ludo and snakes-and-ladders with them as well as joining them in more active pastimes such as hide-and-seek. She taught them to play patience, a card game with which she often whiles away a leisure hour.

Mastery of a few simple conjuring tricks made her, in the eyes of her grandchildren, only a shade less remarkable than the fairy godmother in a pantomime. A favourite trick was one in which she seemed to pass pennies right through her hand so that, empty at the outset, it was suddenly and mystifyingly full of coins. Of course, the children were not completely satisfied until they too knew how it was done.

"I really must learn some more tricks," the Queen Mother confided in a friend. "I simply cannot keep pace with the demand."

A former visitor to Royal Lodge recalls a small dinner party the Queen Mother gave at a time when Charles and Anne were staying there with her. Guests for the dinner party duly arrived, but there was no sign of the Queen Mother. The guests waited and dinner waited. It was nearly an hour later before the royal hostess finally put in a smiling, apologetic appearance. She had, she explained, been reading her grandchildren a bedtime story and quite over-looked the time.

It was the Queen Mother who gave Charles and Anne their first prayer books. She took them to their first pantomime. She took Anne to her first ballet and Charles to his first concert. But he was rather young at the time and fidgeted so restlessly on his velvet cushion that he had to be taken home again before the concert was over.

There were always gifts for them when 'Granny' returned from one of her overseas trips. From America, where she went shopping for the children in such famous New York stores as Saks and Schwartz, Anne received a teenage doll, a toy washing machine and some pretty American-style dresses, while Charles became the proud owner of, among other things, a working model of a steam shovel.

As the two children grew older, Granny's gifts took the form of things of more lasting value. For Charles, on one occasion, there was a silver-framed miniature of 'Granny' to remind him of her in the years to come; for Anne, on another occasion, there was a diamond and ruby brooch, one of her first pieces of jewellery.

But though she dotes on her grandchildren, and there have been times in their lives when she has spoilt them, she has also shown herself an eminently sensible grandmother. She expected them, at this time in their lives, to be as appreciative of small things, such as the picture postcards she sent them from Lundy Island with their special stamps depicting the island's puffin colony, as of expensive and more elaborate gifts purchased along Fifth Avenue.

Between her and Prince Charles there has always existed a rather special relationship, as there often is between a grandmother and the first of her grandchildren. But those who know the Queen Mother insist that it goes deeper than that. It is as though there is much about Prince Charles—his punctiliousness, his occasional stubbornness, the way he carries himself—which reminds her of his grandfather, the late King George VI, the husband to whom she was always so devoted and so deeply attached.

Charles and Anne arrived at Sandringham this particular summer to find that 'Granny' had already left the house to look round the local horticultural show which is held in Sandringham Park each July. They promptly hurried after her and arrived at the show-ground to find her surrounded by the inevitable crowd of onlookers as she toured the exhibits. But for once royal dignity was thrown to the wind as, oblivious of the watching crowd, the two children rushed towards her with an impetus which almost bowled her over, throwing their arms around her to greet her with affectionate hugs and kisses.

They toured the show with her and bought several small gifts—a brooch, a clothes brush and a pair of socks—to take back with them to Buckingham Palace. But the marquee containing various cage-birds intrigued them most and all the way back to Sandringham House they could talk of little else. More than anything else they wanted a lovebird each of their own.

An evening or two later, a local breeder named Potter was working in his garden when one of the royal cars drew up outside.

"It was the biggest shock of my life when I saw the Prince and Princess coming in through the garden gate," Mr. Potter recalls.

Recovering from the sudden shock of surprise, he showed the two royal youngsters round his six aviaries. When they climbed back into the car some time later they had with them a cage containing two lovebirds, paid for by the lady-in-waiting who accompanied them.

The Royal Family have a clever knack for devising unusual names for their pets. A gift horse from the Aga Khan was fittingly named Astrakhan. Two of the earlier royal corgis had been named Carol and Crackers because they were born at Christmas. The children's own corgis were whimsically named Whisky and Sherry. Now the newly-acquired lovebirds became Annie and Davy, so named after two of the children's favourite characters, Davy Crockett and sharp-shooting Annie Oakley of *Annie Get Your Gun* fame.

Wherever the two children went over the next year or so, their beloved lovebirds went with them ... to Windsor, Balmoral, Sandringham. At Buckingham Palace the cage stood in the day nursery, and with Charles away at boarding school, it was Anne's task to clean the cage and feed the lovebirds each day. She tried to teach them various tricks and training reached the stage when they could be allowed out of their cage to fly around the nursery with Annie alighting on a stick which Anne held in her hand. Davy never quite reached that level of proficiency.

But such tricks also had their dangers as became apparent some years later when the lovebirds, on different occasions, were allowed out of their cage with a nursery window inadvertently left open, to head straight for freedom and disappear over the rooftops of London.

A few days after the purchase of the lovebirds the royal children were out shopping again, this time in King's Lynn, a few miles from Sandringham. They each had a pound note to spend as they scrambled excitedly down from the royal car which had brought them into town. They visited a pet store where they bought a climbing ladder and a mirror to furnish the lovebirds' cage. The shopkeeper told them that lovebirds are especially partial to millet; so they bought a spray of that, too.

In another shop, they spent some time looking at the books and toys on display. Princess Anne's mind was soon made up. After leafing through some of the books, she decided instead to buy herself a toy loom. Her brother took things much more seriously. He studied a number of painting sets and some constructional kits for making model aircraft. Then he asked for a toy cricket set to be lifted down from one of the higher shelves so that he could examine it more closely. A mouth-organ was also produced for his inspection.

"Goodness gracious, haven't you chosen yet?" his sister asked him, rather impatiently, at one stage of the proceedings.

But finally Charles made up his mind and elected to buy a bright red water-pistol.

"I want it for shooting frogs," he explained to the shop assistant.

The frogs were presumably those which frequent the lily pond in the grounds of Sandringham House, but the water-pistol was also to come in handy for raiding the kitchen at Balmoral, where, to the amusement of the chefs, one of their number found himself the victim of a well-directed spray of water.

IV

Although she had created her small son Prince of Wales, the Queen continued to take precautions to safeguard him against unnecessary publicity and steadfastly declined to allow him to undertake any royal duties, however minor. Charitable and juvenile organisations seeking the royal patronage of the youthful Prince of Wales were politely turned down. An over-loyal innkeeper who desired to rename his hostelry *The Prince Charles* was discreetly informed that the idea did not meet with royal approval.

Canadian hints that the young Prince should accompany his parents on their forthcoming tour of that vast country fell on deaf ears.

As a Buckingham Palace spokesman explained about that time: "When people suggest that the Prince of Wales should go here, there and everywhere, they are talking as though he is an item of royal cutlery or part of the royal dinner service. He isn't. He is a small boy who has to be educated like any other small boy and continually taking him away from school in this way would seriously interfere with his education."

An elderly widow with a small grandson one year older than Prince Charles wrote to the Queen from her home at Mildenhall.

"How wonderful it would be for other children like my small grandson if Prince Charles could broadcast his own personal message to them once a year. He could tell them all about himself, how he lives, what he does and how he is getting on at school. I am sure the children would love it."

She received a diplomatically-worded reply from Buckingham Palace informing her that her suggestion had been noted. But it was never implemented. The Queen, though she first broadcast herself as a child of fourteen during the war years, had no intention of submitting her son to the ordeal of broadcasting until he was a good deal older.

There were other letters suggesting that Prince Charles should appear on television with his mother when she gave her Christmas Day 'fireside chat' from Sandringham. The Queen did not agree and made some small passing reference to the fact during her next telecast.

"We want our son and daughter to grow up as normally as possible," she told her world-wide audience. "We believe that public life is not a fair burden to place on growing children. I am sure all of you who are parents will understand."

The Queen herself carefully played her part in ensuring that Charles should grow up as 'normally as possible' in his new schoolboy environment at Cheam. She called for no special reports and instituted no special inquiries as to what progress he was making. She wrote to him at Cheam regularly each week, but visited him no more than any other mother might have been expected to visit her son . . . and less than most.

One of her rare visits to Cheam was on the occasion of a school concert when she and Prince Philip joined an audience of other mothers and fathers to hear the boys sing carols and sea shanties and see Charles take part in a humorous sketch entitled *Ten Little Cheam Boys*.

Even when Charles went down with influenza while at Cheam, there was no question of the Queen summoning a royal car and driving post-haste to see how he was. Instead, she had a lady-in-waiting make one or two telephone calls of inquiry and left it at that.

Neither did she go dashing off to Cheam when her son injured his ankle in a fall on the school stairs, the result of some schoolboy skylarking. Charles himself made no fuss about the fall initially, but subsequent examination by the school doctor, Dr. Basil Phillips, showed the ankle to be considerably swollen. Dr. Phillips decided to drive the young Prince, now aged ten, to hospital in nearby Newbury where, following an X-ray examination, the damaged leg was put in plaster.

His leg was still in plaster when Charles went home for his Christmas vacation, a fact which caused Anne to welcome him with a gleeful, "Hi there, Hopalong."

In fact, the whole family were inclined to tease him a bit, on one occasion all hobbling into the room in succession—the Queen, Prince Philip, the Queen Mother and Princess Anne—with imitation stiff legs.

The injured leg was still in plaster when he left to spend Christmas at Sandringham with the rest of the Royal Family and it was during the Christmas stay that he was driven over to King's Lynn hospital to have the plaster cast removed and for a further X-ray check to ascertain that the ankle was making satisfactory progress.

He was keenly interested in everything going on around him at the hospital and, in particular, in knowing something of how the X-ray apparatus worked. He was permitted to watch a farm-worker from the nearby village of Castle Rising having an X-ray examination following a meal of barium, and it came as a considerable surprise to the farm-worker to learn that it was his future King who had been studying his stomach under X-ray.

"I thought it was the son of one of the doctors," he told his wife when he got home.

Again that Christmas, to the children's great delight, there was thick snow in Norfolk and on one occasion when Charles was out with his mother in an estate car they ran into heavy drifts. The Queen is an experienced driver, but the snow that day was too much for her. The car became completely bogged down and there was nothing for it but to trudge to the nearest house and telephone Sandringham for assistance.

At Sandringham, when a feminine voice coming over an outside line announced, "This is the Queen. My car is stuck in the snow and I want you to send another," there was, at first, an inclination to take it for a practical joke. Once they realised that it was, indeed, the Queen speaking, a car was despatched to collect her and Prince Charles and arrangements put in hand for digging out the trapped vehicle.

At Cheam, just as he had the same pocket money as any other boy, so Charles had the same amount of free time . . . no more and no less. Three Sundays in each term he was permitted to spend the day away from school. Sometimes, on these free Sundays, a royal car would arrive to take him and two or three special friends to spend the day at Windsor Castle. On other occasions, he was permitted to visit the home of one of his school-chums, but always with his personal detective tagging along to keep a watchful eye on things. Royalty can unbend only so far.

At Windsor, Charles and his friends would have lunch with his parents and Princess Anne, and, later in the day, would drive over to Royal Lodge for tea with Granny. In between, there would be perhaps a visit to the royal farm, to the stables to see the horses, or an impromptu game of football on the golf course with folded coats acting as goalposts. From time to time Prince Philip would join in the game of football, as would Princess Anne.

"Football isn't a game for girls," her brother protested on one occasion. Nevertheless, the fleet-footed Anne proved that she could more than hold her own with the boys.

During one of these Sunday visits to Windsor Castle it was suggested that the young Prince should entertain his school friends by showing them round the State rooms with their valuable paintings and ancient furnishings. But paintings and furniture were to prove less attractive to the schoolboy mind than armour and weapons and what started out as a quiet tour of inspection ended as a boisterous game of 'storming the castle', involving some considerable scuffling and shouting among the small cannon at the top of one of the stairways.

At Balmoral, in summer, Anne's company, these days, was augmented during part of the holiday by the presence of one of Prince Charles' school friends. Such visits brought their reasonable quota of boyhood adventures and occasional disagreements, and a former royal servant has revealed in an interview published in the United States that one disagreement between the Prince and a holiday friend over whose turn it was to ride the bicycle they were sharing ended in a bout of boyish pummelling.

Boyhood jokes were becoming a shade more sophisticated. The day before America's President Eisenhower was due to visit the Queen at Balmoral, the young Prince was glimpsed walking around wearing a home-made badge bearing the slogan: I Like Ike.

Another, less important visitor to Balmoral about this time remembers leaving his hat and coat just outside the door of the royal equerry's room. He emerged from the room some time later to find that they were now adorning the statue of Queen Victoria's consort, Prince Albert, which adjoins the stairway in the main hall. It is difficult to think of anyone at Balmoral outside the schoolboy Prince who would have perpetrated such a joke.

But inside the schoolboy there was always the Prince, increasingly conscious of his special position. The story is told of how Charles and a small party of school friends were travelling in one of the royal cars between Cheam and Windsor. The young Prince was recognised and people waved. Prince Charles duly waved back.

One of his schoolboy companions is said to have passed some comment on this exchange of salutations between Prince and people, to which Charles replied, "When people wave at me, it is only polite to wave back."

10   *The Sporting Instinct*

I

Prince Charles was ten when he shot his first grouse on the heather-clad moors of Balmoral. On his return to Balmoral Castle at the end of the day, he ran excitedly into the kitchen with his 'bag', asking the chef to cook the bird for his supper.

From childhood, the future King has been brought up in the fishin' and shootin' tradition of the English country gentleman, perhaps not surprisingly since his recent ancestors, Edward VII, George V and George VI, were all among the outstanding shots of their day, as Prince Philip is now.

His mother, the Queen, was raised in the same outdoor tradition. She was only a young girl when she shot her first stag and in the years which followed one of her favourite pursuits when staying at Balmoral was to don a knickerbocker suit, take a packed lunch and set off in pursuit of a stag with only a solitary gillie for company. She would tramp up steep hills, wade streams and negotiate bogs in the long cross-country pursuit of the quarry, invariably felling it with a single shot once she had it in the sights of her rifle.

While the Queen has largely forsaken the hunting rifle for the camera in more recent years, Prince Philip has stepped into the royal tradition. Philip had little enthusiasm for or knowledge of shooting when he first stayed at Sandringham and Balmoral with the Royal Family. His first-ever visit to Balmoral found him without the tweeds normally worn for shooting and he accompanied his prospective father-in-law, the late King George VI, over the heathery moors clad in flannel trousers and a sweater. Subsequently, at Sandringham, if local countryfolk can be believed, he was chided by the King on one occasion when they were out shooting together.

But shooting was a basic part of the royal tradition and Philip was firmly resolved to master it, a resolution he carried through so well that once, in Denmark, he achieved the feat of bringing down twelve pheasants with thirteen shots.

Prince Charles' first introduction to the shooting field came early on, when, as a small boy, he accompanied his mother to watch the guns in action. Boy-like, he imitated what his father did, putting a stick and, later, a toy gun to his shoulder and shouting "Bang-bang" as the birds flew overhead. He helped the beaters in their task of rounding up the birds and also helped to count the bag at the end of the day.

Just as he had taught him to swim in the palace pool, so his father now took him in hand and taught him how to shoot. At Balmoral, in the summer of 1959, Charles got in his first serious practice with a shotgun. He also had his own gundog, a black labrador named Flash from the royal kennels at Sandringham. (His father's dog was a yellow labrador named Candy.)

But Prince Charles, only ten at this time, was perhaps not yet of an age to achieve the full mastery of man over dog and Flash, with a canine instinct for such things, doubtless recognised the fact. There was an occasion, early on in their relationship, when Charles was trying to persuade the dog to get into a waiting Land Rover in readiness to set off for a day's sport. But Flash declined to comply. Unable to persuade the dog to obey his spoken commands, Charles tried to catch hold of him to demonstrate what was wanted. It was a mistake. Taking the boy's action for the beginning of some glorious game, Flash bounded away, darting this way and that with his young master in pursuit.

The Queen came out of the castle at that moment, took in the situation and uttered a loud whistle which brought Flash obediently to heel.

At Sandringham, over Christmas, as part of the boy's training in the manly arts, Prince Philip took his son with him when taking part in the annual coot shoot organised by Major Aubrey Buxton at Hickling Broad. Charles' participation on that occasion consisted mainly of helping to retrieve the dead birds from the water or among the reeds with the aid of a long-handled angling net. Father and son were again at Hickling the following year and the year after that, stopping off on this last occasion on their way back from attending the wedding of Lady Pamela Mountbatten. It was a period of particularly rugged weather which at times reached almost blizzard proportions, and they spent the night at the Pleasure Boat Inn, where Prince Charles shared a room with Major Buxton's son and another small boy. Despite the severity of the weather, the young Prince was out with the shooting party in the morning, but for the afternoon the boys preferred to remain indoors watching football on television.

It was not to be expected that the future King's induction in the art of shooting would go either unnoticed or uncriticised, and there was to be, later, a protest from the League Against Cruel Sports at the news that Charles, in company with his father and a school friend, Norton Knatchbull, the son of Lord Brabourne, had been out after pheasants with a .410 shotgun. There was a further outburst when Charles was reported as having shot his first stag on the moors at Balmoral, a deed which was 'vigorously condemned' in a resolution which the League sent to the Queen.

Just as he was teaching his son to shoot, so Prince Philip, around this time, began to initiate him into the game of polo. He had a miniature polo mallet made for the boy and at weekends, if Charles was home from Cheam, the two of them would go out into the Home Park at Windsor and manoeuvre round each other on bicycles, taking swings at a polo ball, a procedure not without its occasional spill.

Charles also practised on a mechanical polo horse which his father had had installed to help improve his own game, an ingenious arrangement of slopes and nets returning the ball after each shot. Later he graduated to a real polo pony, San Quinina, a chestnut mare from the Argentine which his father passed on to him by way of encouragement. Later still came another pony, Sombra, a gift from Lord Cowdray.

His father, supervising one of his early practice sessions on San Quinina, consoled him with the remark, "It takes time to get the knack." Prince Philip should know. He has been playing polo since his naval days in Malta, back in 1950, and ranks today as one of Britain's foremost players.

It wasn't until he was at Gordonstoun, during the school holidays, that Charles played his first real game of polo. In company with two other young novices, he played in a team captained by his father against a similarly inexperienced team under the captaincy of Colonel W. H. Gerard Leigh, chairman of the Household Brigade Polo Club. He rode both his ponies, San Quinina and Sombra, in turn and had the thrill of scoring his first-ever goal from the saddle of San Quinina.

Charles, of course, was familiar with horses long before he ever mounted his first polo pony. Indeed, he was learning to ride before he went to school. He learned to ride on a small, borrowed Shetland pony. The Shetland was followed by William, a strawberry roan from Ireland, and then by Greensleeves, a chestnut roan from Wales. Early lessons on a leading rein were followed by gentle trots across Windsor Great Park, his instructor close beside him and, later, by weekend rides with his mother.

Princess Anne learned to ride in the same fashion and at Windsor, on Saturday mornings, the two of them would share a half-hour lesson together, before going riding with their mother. Sometimes, on these occasions, there was a brief period of waiting between the end of the lesson and the Queen's appearance. When that happened, Charles and Anne would pit their ponies one against the other in a dash across the castle golf course. Truth requires the admission that the future King, in those days before he graduated to polo ponies, usually lost to his more impetuous younger sister.

Like her mother, the Queen, Princess Anne has always been completely at ease with horses, completely at home in the saddle. Indeed, when it comes to riding, Anne seems to have inherited both her mother's enthusiasm and a large degree of the dash and daring her father exhibits on the polo field. These days, Anne's high spirits on horseback are channelled into junior riding and jumping competitions in which she has had a not inconsiderable degree of success. But, earlier on, her enthusiasm found other, more unofficial, outlets.

At Balmoral one summer a series of wild yells and whoops brought everyone—servants and members of the Royal Family alike—rushing to the windows. They were greeted by the spectacle of Princess Anne, decked out in a magnificent Indian headdress her royal parents had brought her back from one visit to Canada, galloping bareback round and round the front lawn until her mother intervened and told her to take the pony back to the stables to be saddled properly.

But there was one occasion at Balmoral when Anne's daring and impetuosity resulted in a fall. It was a domestic custom at Balmoral at this time for servants to erect a short length of line near the trees of a small copse at the rear of the castle so that newly-laundered linen could hang in the fresh air without being an eyesore. On this occasion, Anne came galloping out of the copse in her customary impetuous fashion and failed to notice the line in position. It caught her across the body and jerked her from the saddle. Fortunately she was unhurt apart from a shaking and some bruising. She climbed to her feet, collected her pony, which had meantime come to a well-trained standstill, and swung herself back into the saddle.

At Windsor one of her favourite tricks was to put her pony into a gallop and head for the high wall which separates the royal gardens from the park beyond. To anyone who was watching, as the Queen was on at least one occasion, it must have seemed as though she was going to try to jump the wall, a dangerous feat. Then, at almost the last moment, she would swerve her pony to one side and bring it to a standstill.

At Sandringham as a joke, she once tried to ride her pony up the stone steps of the main entrance, as the adjutant does at Sandhurst Military College on the day of the annual passing-out parade. Displaying perhaps rather more sense than his young mistress, her pony firmly declined to have anything to do with the experiment. Dismounting, Anne tried to lead him up the steps, but even the help of the Queen Mother, who entered into the spirit of the occasion, could not persuade the pony to emulate the Sandhurst example.

For Charles, in addition to shooting and polo, there was also early tuition from his father in the manly arts of handling a boat and driving a car. At Balmoral, father and son would go over to Loch Muick for trips in a racing catamaran and at Cowes, when he was not yet nine, Charles had his first experience of actual racing when he and the veteran yachtsman, Uffa Fox, acted as crew to Prince Philip aboard the royal Dragon-class *Bluebottle*. Charles' biggest thrill came after the race when he was permitted to take the helm and steer the craft back to the royal yacht *Britannia*.

He raced with his father in *Bluebottle* again the following day and also accompanied him aboard the twenty-four-footer, *Fairey Fox,* in a friendly race against the other three royal craft, *Bluebottle, Coweslip* and *White Heron*. This race had a somewhat unexpected outcome, with *Fairey Fox* shipping so much water that frantic baling was called for and it was deemed advisable for Charles to be taken off. However, the situation was not really serious and the schoolboy Charles regarded it as a huge lark, as he did on another occasion when his father took him out in a motor boat which unfortunately broke down, with the result that they had to be towed back to Uffa Fox's waterside home.

For the young Prince—and, indeed, for his father—an intriguing diversion at Uffa Fox's home took the form of an ancient motor horn which it was customary to hide under a cushion for some unsuspecting visitor to sit upon. Prince Philip, on one of his early visits, had been tricked in this fashion and subsequently took royal delight in catching other visitors in the same manner.

Prince Charles had his first experience of handling a car at a very tender age, sitting on his father's lap to turn the steering wheel while Prince Philip's considerably longer legs manipulated the necessary pedals. Later came two nippy little 80 c.c. go-karts with two-stroke engines in which he and Anne—and sometimes Prince Philip—would race each other round the private roads of the various royal estates. Charles was practising in his go-kart at Sandringham one day when he skidded on the gravel near the front door and ploughed his way into the rose bed which edges the lawn. After that, the go-karts were carefully tuned to a maximum of twelve miles an hour and Prince Philip also ordered the two youngsters to wear safety helmets.

By the time he was twelve, and long before he was old enough to qualify for a driving licence, Charles was already sufficiently expert as a driver to take the wheel of a Land Rover and drive his father some six miles along the private roads of the royal estate at Balmoral on a visit to the Queen Mother at Birkhall. Anne, nearly two years younger, drove her mother in similar fashion, though, to comply with the law at one point of the route where it involved a short stretch of public highway, parents and children changed places at the wheels of their respective vehicles.

Fishing was another pastime which involved Prince Charles' attention. His interest was first aroused as he watched Granny—the Queen Mother—casting for salmon in the tumbling waters of the River Dee. She went with him to a shop in Ballater to select some of his first fishing tackle and after that, sometimes with his father and sometimes under the watchful eye of a trusted gillie, he would go fishing in the streams and lochs around Balmoral, usually returning with two or three small trout which he would take to the kitchen with a request to the chef to cook them for his supper or breakfast. On other occasions, if the family were out for a picnic at some favourite spot along the shores of Loch Muick, father and son would cook their catch on the spot with the portable barbecue.

II

Exposure to schoolboy life also exposed the future King to schoolboy ailments and schoolboy bumps and bruises. Since going to Cheam he had already gone down with a dose of 'flu and sustained a sprained ankle. Then, at Easter, 1959, he came home from school with a bout of chicken-pox which he promptly passed on to Princess Anne.

Notwithstanding such minor ailments and mishaps, the Queen and Prince Philip were content that, in other ways, the big experiment of sending the future King to boarding school was working out successfully. By and large, the newspapers had ceased to inquire so closely into his schoolday deeds and misdeeds, the photographers had moved on to new and more fruitful pastures with their tele-photo lenses, and sightseers no longer descended quite so numerously on Cheam and the surrounding district at weekends. So delighted were the royal parents with the way things were working out that they raised the possibility of sending Princess

Anne similarly to boarding school, a prospect the young Princess hailed with enthusiasm.

During the Royal Family's customary Easter stay at Windsor Castle, Prince Charles was taken on a visit to St. George's Chapel to see the seat he would one day occupy as a Knight of the Garter. He also had a look round Eton College, a fact which was taken by some as evidence that he would one day go there, and was also permitted by his parents to go shopping in Windsor itself. A newspaper account that there was a queue waiting to see round St. George's Chapel at the time of his visit and that an attendant, failing to recognise him, told him he must wait his turn in line seems improbable.

He continued his earlier explorations of Windsor Castle with a growing consciousness of its ancient history and significance, but his outlook was perhaps still more that of boyhood than of future monarchy, at least judging by one remark he is reported to have made. In the Grand Corridor of the castle, close to the Queen's private sitting room, hangs a painting of King Charles I. Executed by Van Dyck to enable the Italian sculptor, Giovanni Bernini, to fashion a bust of the king, it is a triple portrait of left profile, full face and right profile.

But the future King Charles III's reaction to this work of art was typically schoolboyish. "Who's the fellow with three heads?" he is said to have asked.

He turned up, unexpected and unannounced, in all parts of the castle and a burly sergeant-major in the Irish Guards found himself bawling a hoarse-throated, "On your feet, men," when the ten-year-old Prince walked unheralded into the guardroom one day. To the delight of the men on guard duty, the young Prince, before leaving again, employed a pocket-knife to carve his name on the guardroom wall as a souvenir of his visit.

With his mother and sister, he went along to watch his father playing polo at Smith's Lawn, helping to look after his father's polo ponies and running on to the field between chukkas to stamp down divots kicked up by the flashing hooves of the ponies during the game. It was with considerable schoolboy pride that he handed his father his polo stick as he trotted out on to the field and he was ready, waiting, with a bottle of water to cool his father's thirst at the end of a chukka. Hotter than usual on one occasion, Prince Philip showed his son a quick way to cool off. He up-ended the water bottle and poured the contents over his head.

Much as the sport of polo intrigued the future King, there were, inevitably, times when his attention wandered to more schoolboy delights. Such was the occasion on a May day of driving rain. The rainwater collected in puddles on the roof of the royal tent and Charles devised a new diversion. He jumped up and down, hitting the canvas with his hand, scattering the rainwater puddles in a shower of spray. Then his mother intervened and told him to stop it.

Cheam apart, he was getting a more varied and down-to-earth upbringing than any heir to the Throne had ever known before. More and more, even if the fact went unnoticed by the general public at the time, his royal parents were letting him go out and about, in London as well as at Windsor. That summer, early in the school holidays, before going to Balmoral for the customary summer stay, he went to the London Casino to see the Cinerama show, *The Seven Wonders of the World,* to the London Planetarium in Baker Street and to Battersea Fun Fair, where for an hour and a half he enjoyed himself on the dodgem cars, in the mirror maze and on one of the houp-la stalls. As an end-of-holidays treat, before returning to Cheam, he was taken to Pinewood Studios where he watched the filming of a scene for *Sink the Bismarck.* Always interested in the mechanical side of things, as his father is, he studied the film cameras with considerable interest and talked with the cameramen before moving on to another sound stage where he saw a convent scene being filmed for *Conspiracy of Hearts* and met film stars Sylvia Sims, Lilli Palmer and Yvonne Mitchell.

But the more serious side of his upbringing was by no means neglected and as part of his out-of-school training for future monarchy he went also that holiday time to the Houses of Parliament and Westminster Abbey, where he will one day go again as the main actor in the ancient ceremony of Coronation.

III

Among other things, Prince Charles had improved considerably in his command of the French language during the time he had been at Cheam. But his mother considered it important that he should speak it with something of her own fluency and to this end she invited a twenty-seven-year-old French-Canadian, Lieutenant Jean Lajeunesse, a graduate of Montreal University, to stay at Balmoral that summer.

The Queen, just back from another royal tour of Canada, had in fact first met Lieutenant Lajeunesse on a previous visit to that country. Prince Charles, by now, was well accustomed to his parents' enforced absences on their various overseas tours and was preoccupied at school when they flew out to Newfoundland at the start of their latest trip . . . a strenuous 45-day, 16,000-mile journey which was to take them right across Canada, from the Atlantic to the Pacific and as far north as the Yukon . . . but he was taken to London Airport to meet them on their return and may perhaps, in his schoolboy fashion, have noticed how pale and strained his mother was looking.

Five days after she arrived back from Canada, the Queen, after an examination by two of the royal physicians, left for Balmoral with her husband and the two children. More than ever this summer she needed a long, relaxing break from royal routine, as evidenced by the official announcement she left behind her at Buckingham Palace for public release as soon as she and her family were safely secluded amidst the vast, heathery acres of their Highland home.

It was an announcement which began with the time-honoured phrase: "The Queen will undertake no further public engagements . . ."

It was the first official intimation, though there had been rumours in plenty, that the Queen was expecting another baby.

But the ten-year-old future King was not yet privy to his mother's personal secret as the royal train travelled north to Scotland. The Queen confided in Mabel Anderson, who had charge of the children, during the course of the journey. Miss Anderson, of course, was delighted that, with Charles now at boarding school and talk of

Anne shortly to follow suit, there was soon to be another small occupant to keep the royal nursery lively and busy. But the Queen impressed upon her that she was not to tell Charles and Anne about the expected baby. That was a pleasure she was reserving for herself.

She told them over lunch that first day at Balmoral. They were both so excited at the unexpected news that they did scant justice to the meal and could hardly wait in their eagerness to get back to the nursery and tell Miss Anderson and others of the nursery staff all about it. Miss Anderson, of course, listened to them as attentively as though this was the first intimation she had received.

Another member of the staff asked the two children which they wanted—a baby brother or a baby sister.

Charles, at least, had not the slightest doubt on that score.

"A brother, of course," he declared with a schoolboy's lofty contempt for girls.

Echoing Charles, Anne, too, voted for another brother.

I I   *"Jolly Good"*

I

Back at Cheam that autumn, Prince Charles found himself promoted to the captaincy of the junior football team. His early efforts at soccer had been mainly in the forward line, but he had revealed himself a robust rather than speedy player and was playing now at right full-back, a position where he proved himself a staunch defender who had few inhibitions about the possibility of coming off second best in a tackle. But even on the football field he could not altogether restrain his innate sense of politeness and the effect of a doughty tackle was occasionally offset by a brief pause in the proceedings while Prince Charles helped a tumbled opponent to his feet and apologised for his own robustness.

He was also busy in the school workshop around this time on a new project, the rocking elephant with a padded red saddle which was his personal gift to his new baby brother, Prince Andrew.

The approaching birth of the new baby had necessarily involved a move-round in the royal nursery at Buckingham Palace. Until now, on the infrequent occasions when he slept at home these days, Prince Charles had continued to occupy the same nursery bedroom he had had since babyhood, though he had, of course, outgrown any necessity to have a nanny sleeping in the same room. That practice had long since been discontinued. Now, with Princess Anne's bedroom being readied as a night nursery for the new baby, Anne moved into Charles' room, taking her pet possessions and favourite books (mainly to do with horses) along with her. To make way for her, Charles moved out of the nursery suite altogether. Now he had a room of his own quite detached from the nursery suite, though still on the same floor, at the front of the palace.

The Queen's pregnancy prevented her from attending the

wedding of Lady Pamela Mountbatten and interior decorator David Hicks in the January of 1960. But Prince Charles, wearing a new suit, travelled from Sandringham to Romsey Abbey for the wedding in the company of his father and Princess Anne. For him, it was a doubly important occasion. Although he had raced about often enough at holiday times in jeans and corduroys, this was the first occasion on which he had had a suit with long trousers.

But long trousers do not necessarily turn a schoolboy into a man, nor does a champagne glass containing a soft drink with which to toast the health of the bride and bridegroom, and when a snowstorm blew up during the wedding reception at the Mountbatten residence Charles was still sufficient of a boy to remark that it was 'jolly good weather' for tobogganing.

The Christmas holidays were over and he was back at Cheam when his baby brother, Prince Andrew, was born at Buckingham Palace on February 17. A royal car was despatched to Cheam to fetch him to the palace where the new baby lay snuggled in the same frill-trimmed cot which Charles himself had occupied some eleven years earlier.

That year of 1960 continued to be one of event and excitement for the young Prince. Close on the heels of the birth of Prince Andrew came the fuss and excitement of 'Margo's wedding' to the energetic and talented young photographer who is now Lord Snowdon.

We cannot vouch for the story that Prince Charles demanded, "Whatever would the chaps at Cheam think?" when it was suggested that he should don knee-breeches and buckle shoes to serve as a pageboy at his aunt's wedding, but it is hardly more unlikely than the Duke of Windsor's own account of how concern as to what his contemporaries might think caused him to have youthful doubts about the elaborate costume he was required to wear for his ceremonial installation as Prince of Wales.

In between these two historic events . . . the birth of a baby Prince and the marriage of a Princess . . . came something of less historic importance which was yet, to Prince Charles, perhaps more exciting than either. It was a visit to Scotland Yard, where he had his fingerprints taken (as his father did when he visited the Yard), met a police dog named Amigo and his handler, Constable Ronald Jackson, and was privileged to watch what was going on in the Information Room, nerve-centre of the Yard's fight against crime.

The occupants of police car Alpha 15 were cruising along the Thames Embankment, carrying out a routine patrol, when a somewhat youthful voice came over the car radio.

"This is M.P." (call-sign for the Metropolitan Police) "calling Alpha 15. Proceed at once to the North Extension car park and pick me up."

Alpha 15 did as instructed. It collected Prince Charles, who had Princess Anne along with him, and took the two youngsters on patrol along the Embankment as far as Lambeth Bridge, from where Charles called up Scotland Yard on the car's radio: "This is Alpha 15 calling M.P. Am now returning."

The process of finger-printing appears to have made the biggest impression on his young mind and a former member of the palace staff remembers that the young Prince borrowed an ink pad subsequently to demonstrate how it was done.

The Easter holidays that year also included the customary royal visit to the Badminton horse trials, though Prince Charles was perhaps more enthused over the jet speedboat which was being tried out on the lake.

"Jolly good," he commented with schoolboy enthusiasm after being taken out for a trip in the boat. Almost inevitably, his next remark was, "May I have a try, please?" and off he went again, piloting the craft at a speed of about fifteen knots with an admiring younger sister as passenger.

That summer the Queen paid one of her rare visits to her son's school at Cheam, presenting the prizes at the annual prize-giving ceremony, among them one to Prince Charles for improved proficiency at French. During his mother's visit to the school he also had a bookshelf on show in the carpentry display and came equal first in one of the swimming events included in the day's programme. And the following term he was to gain his cycling proficiency badge, another small milestone along the road of schooldays.

During the school holidays, whether at Buckingham Palace,

Sandringham or Balmoral, he and Anne continued to be close companions. They may not, at this stage of their lives, have been quite so inseparable as they were once, but they were still often together.

On the Queen Mother's birthday, after going along to Clarence House to take Granny the birthday gifts they had bought for her, they went to see the Hayley Mills film *Pollyanna* at Studio One in Oxford Street.

The cinema commissionaire, busy ushering hordes of holiday-going youngsters into the building with cries of "Hurry along there" was doubtless surprised to recognise the Queen's children amongst them. He was perhaps even more surprised when Prince Charles gave him a boyish wink of friendly acknowledgement.

The two youngsters paid eight and sixpence each to sit in the front row of the circle. "It was jolly good, wasn't it?" Charles was reported as saying to his sister as they came out of the cinema at the end of the film.

The remark has the ring of authenticity. It was a schoolboy expression, doubtless acquired at Cheam, which he tended to use rather a lot around this time. Everything of which he approved—from jet speedboats to snowy weather for tobogganing, from Hayley Mills to the Bolshoi Ballet (which he visited in company with the Queen Mother)—was 'jolly good'.

Oxford Street was crowded with home-going shoppers and busy with rush-hour traffic when the two royal youngsters emerged from Studio One and a director of the cinema dashed loyally into the road and held up traffic so that they could cross safely to a waiting car.

Another cinema visit was to see the film *Ben Hur* in a programme which also included a documentary entitled *Princess Margaret: This Is Your Life*. The two children again sat in the dress circle and afterwards they walked along the street with Miss Peebles, Anne's governess, until they could hail a passing cabby and give him the address: "Buckingham Palace, please."

Like most schoolboys, Prince Charles seemed to have developed the ability to eat the most indigestible mixtures at almost any conceivable time and at Knebworth, during a car journey to

Sandringham, he popped into a shop to buy two pork-pies and a packet of cocktail biscuits. The detective accompanying him queried the wisdom of such a mixture, saying that the cocktail biscuits had cream in them.

"It isn't cream, is it?" Charles appealed to the shopkeeper. "It's cheese, isn't it?"

The weather was mainly fine and sunny at Sandringham that summer and on really hot days Charles and Anne would be driven over to Holkham to swim from a private beach belonging to the Earl and Countess of Leicester. The Countess, formally styled Lady of the Bedchamber, is one of the Queen's ladies-in-waiting.

Later that year there was an outburst of criticism from the Lord's Day Observance Society, directed perhaps more at Princess Margaret than Charles and Anne, when the two youngsters were treated to some ice cream during a Sunday visit to the Norfolk village of Burnham Market.

"Where is the example?" demanded the Society's quarterly magazine. "In which direction are the children being led?"

Amplifying this criticism, the Society's secretary was reported as saying, "Once the royal children go out and buy ice cream on a Sunday, every child in the country will think it is right to do the same."

Prince Charles was still a year short of his teens, but the fact did not prevent various magazines from speculating from time to time concerning his romantic future, with the youngest of the three princesses of Denmark, Princess Anne-Marie, still a firm favourite as England's possible future queen. By contrast with the magazines, the newspapers seemed more concerned with the continued unruliness of his brown hair, a concern which may well have been shared by his mother, the Queen, judging by one story told around this time. She is said to have teased him with looking like 'a Shetland pony'.

Be that as it may, with so many boyhood activities to be squeezed into the holiday at Balmoral that summer, Charles seems to have missed his customary holiday haircut from the local barber at Ballater and his return to Buckingham Palace with his brown locks clearly in need of attention resulted in an urgent S.O.S. to a discreet, long-established hairdressing concern in Curzon Street. Shortly afterwards a man's hairdresser arrived at the palace to give the young Prince a much-needed 'short back and sides' to fit him for his return to the schoolboy world of Cheam.

"I must say it was a little long," the hairdresser, his task done, commented diplomatically. "Needed a trim."

II

November 14, 1961—a Tuesday—was a significant day in the life of the future King. It was his thirteenth birthday. A single day, of course, does not involve a mystical transformation from boy to teenager, but nevertheless Prince Charles was moving, however imperceptibly, from the carefree, happy-go-lucky world of childhood and boyhood into the difficult, awkward, uncertain teenage years.

For Charles, at school at Cheam, the day passed much like any other. School rules permitted birthday parties to be held only on Wednesdays and Sundays.

That Christmas, almost as though in recognition of the transition from boy to teenager, he went not to a pantomime or circus but to the American musical, *The Sound of Music*. It was not, admittedly, his first more grown-up show. The previous April he and Anne had been taken to see those slapstick comics, the Crazy Gang, sitting in the fifth row of the stalls and munching chocolates between laughs.

At Sandringham that Christmas the young Prince was equally considered sufficient of an adult to become a member of one of his father's shooting parties for a day among the pheasants. "He's getting to be a pretty fair shot," commented one gamekeeper who observed the way the young Prince handled both himself and his gun. But a few days later it was the schoolboy rather than the Prince who called at the station bookstall in nearby King's Lynn in anticipation of purchasing two of his favourite comics. But the comics were not in stock and he contented himself with buying two schoolboy paperbacks instead.

Even on holiday his education continued, though mostly

The young Prince begins to learn about sailing aboard the yacht "Bluebottle" in a Dragon Class race during the 1957 Cowes Week (*above*) and eight years later, also at the Cowes Week Regatta, he seems very much a good crewman for his father on the Royal yawl "Bloodhound".

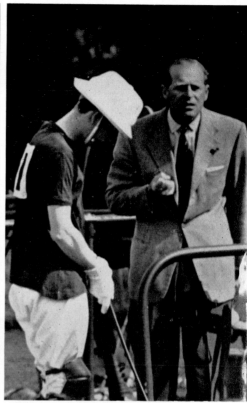

Opposite. While Prince Philip was playing in the opening polo game of the 1962 season at Windsor, his son mounted a pony to practice nearby. Under the watchful eye of a groom, he essayed his first tentative strokes.

This page. Now a seasoned player with his own team, Prince Charles listens to a persuasive argument on strategy from his father.

This page. As the guest of Prince Franz Josef II of Liechtenstein, Prince Charles spent his winter sports holiday at Vaduz Castle. The seventeen year old Prince dons his skis at Malbunan. (*below*) Takes his sister for a tobogga ride.

KEYSTONE PRESS

Opposite page, top. Princess Anne and Prince Charles glare at the unauthorized photographer who managed to get away with this picture. The others were royally dumped into the sea by Prince Charles and Prince Gustaf of Sweden.

CAMERA PRESS

Opposite below. Wielding a bow saw with his Timbertop schoolmate Stuart McGregor, Prince Charles displays a natural healthy zest for life in the Australian bush.

KEYSTONE PRESS

Before the Queen and the Duke of Edinburgh and the parents of students at Gordonstoun, the Prince of Wales gives an outstanding performance as Macbeth. Handsomely bearded, he looks every inch a king, as he enacts the famous Dagger Scene.

Athens, Greece. Britain's Prince Charles leaves the Metropolitan
Basilica of the Annunciation with three other European Princes with
whom he acted as "Best Man" at the wedding of King Constantine of
Greece and Princess Anne-Marie of Denmark.

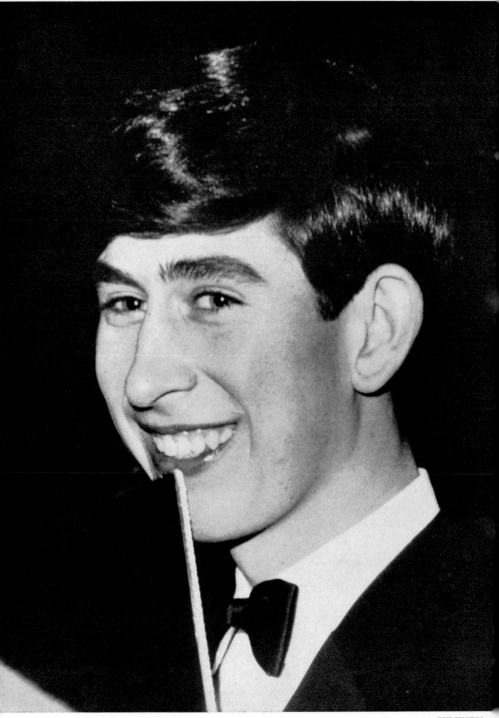

A smiling and extremely grown up Prince Charles is pictured above at an evening function in January, 1966, just before leaving Britain to continue his education in Australia.

enjoyably. During that Christmas stay at Sandringham he was taken to a King's Lynn factory to watch the process by which beet is converted into sugar, and he also visited the town's ancient guildhall where he displayed keen interest in the modern lighting equipment which had been installed for stage productions.

A few months later found him attending his first dance. Wearing a grey suit, he escorted his sister, Princess Anne, to the Garth Hunt Pony Club ball in the White Hart Hotel at Windsor. Accompanied by one of the royal ladies-in-waiting, the two of them arrived at the dance around half-past eight and stayed for about three hours. The 150 others attending the dance were mainly young people and the royal youngsters enjoyed themselves equally with everyone else. The always exuberant Anne delighted in the Twist and Charles found his early dancing lessons, coupled with classes in ballroom dancing at Cheam, standing him in good stead as he tackled the intricacies of the Charleston, the Gay Gordons and a lively Eightsome Reel.

In between these two occasions—the pheasant shoot at Sandringham and the Pony Club dance at Windsor—came a period of considerable discomfort for the young Prince and considerable concern for his royal parents. He awoke in his dormitory at Cheam one Sunday morning feeling decidedly unwell. He was seen by the school matron, who wisely decided to call in the school doctor, Dr. Basil Phillips. Dr. Phillips, in turn, decided to seek the counsel of Sir Wilfrid Sheldon. Sir Wilfrid, whose work on *Diseases of Infancy and Childhood* is generally recognised as the standard British textbook on paediatrics, has watched over the health of the royal children since Charles was a baby.

Now, on receipt of the summons from Dr. Phillips, he drove immediately to Cheam from his home in Surrey and, together, he and Dr. Phillips diagnosed appendicitis. Prince Philip was away touring South America and the Queen was spending her customary weekend at Windsor. She was informed of her son's condition and that evening, with the boy's stomach pains becoming increasingly severe, she gave her consent to an operation. A cable went off to South America to inform Prince Philip of what was happening.

Late that night the future King was carried out to the waiting ambulance on a stretcher. Arrangements had been made for the appendectomy to be performed at the Great Ormond Street Hospital for Sick Children in London and the resident surgeon, David Waterston, had already been alerted at his home at Isleworth. Sir John Joyce, surgeon at the nearby hospital in Newbury, had also been called in.

It was already after midnight when the ambulance arrived at Great Ormond Street, after the fifty-six-mile journey from Cheam, and at half-past two in the morning came news that all was well. It took the form of a bulletin signed by Sir Wilfrid Sheldon, Dr. Phillips, Dr. Margaret Hawksley (the anaesthetist), Sir John Joyce and Mr. David Waterston: "H.R.H. the Prince of Wales underwent an operation for acute appendicitis early this morning. His condition is satisfactory."

The Queen, of course, had been kept informed of her son's condition and a further cable went off to Prince Philip, who was staying at the time on a ranch some eighty miles from the Venezuelan capital of Caracas. Assured that all was well, Prince Philip decided that there was no need to cancel or alter the remainder of his tour schedule, though he made arrangements for a fatherly chat with his son in hospital. To this end, post office engineers were called in to run a cable in through the window of Charles' seventh-floor bedroom and instal a telephone at his bedside. The young Prince was occupying the same room which his sister, Anne, had occupied when she had her tonsils removed some two years before. Unobtrusively, a royal detective took up temporary residence in an adjoining room.

The Queen drove to the hospital that afternoon to visit her young son, taking with her a large basket of fruit as well as a bunch of freshly-cut flowers from the gardens at Windsor. But Charles, she found, was still restricted to a liquid diet and, in any event, felt little like eating.

His mother remained with him for some time, sitting at his bedside, chatting. A cup of tea was brought to her and, leaving the hospital some time later, she exchanged reassuring smiles with other mothers who were visiting their children.

Charles' stay in hospital was further relieved by a visit from Anne and Andrew and by visits from 'Granny' and 'Margo'—the Queen Mother and Princess Margaret.

Out of hospital again, with Prince Philip still away in South America, Charles took his father's place at the next royal luncheon party to be held at Buckingham Palace. He was still looking somewhat pale after his recent operation as he walked into the Bow Room, where the guests were assembled, in the company of his mother, the Queen Mother and Princess Marina. During the meal which followed he helped to uphold the royal end in conversation with such notables as the chairman of the British Broadcasting Corporation, a former chairman of the Trades Union Congress, the editor of the .Church Times, and choreographer Frederick Ashton.

Bit by bit, as opportunity served and as she deemed advisable, the Queen was introducing the future King to the threshold of public life. She had, earlier, during a Christmas visit to Sandringham, permitted him to read one of the Lessons during a carol service held in the nearby village church at West Newton. But she was not yet—and perhaps more than ever now—prepared to submit him to the ordeal of public life which would have been his lot had she acceded to even one-tenth of the requests concerning the young Prince which continued to be received at Buckingham Palace. Only a few months earlier, for all that he was Duke of Cornwall, she had politely, but firmly, declined to let him perform the opening ceremony of a new bridge linking the counties of Devon and Cornwall.

The after-effects of the boy's appendicectomy did not linger long and a short time after leaving hospital Charles was following in his sister's footsteps with visits to Richmond ice stadium. Warmly clad in grey flannels and a fawn sweater, tightly clutching the arm of instructress Betty Calloway, he took his first uncertain steps at ice skating. The skating lesson lasted seventy-five minutes, with a brief break for tea and chocolate biscuits, and by his third lesson Charles was making sufficient progress to forgo the reassuring arm of the instructress.

As a special 'get well' treat, his mother took him and two school-friends, Charles Donald and Christopher Wilson, to watch the

Royal Navy *v.* Royal Air Force rugby football game at Twickenham and afterwards all three boys went back with the Queen for tea at Windsor Castle. Another enjoyable schoolboy outing at this time was a visit to Broadcasting House where Charles watched members of the cast rehearsing a realistic cops-and-robbers episode for the weekly television programme, *Z Cars*.

A warm reunion between father and son marked Prince Philip's return from his South American tour and that weekend Charles and his mother were again at Smith's Lawn to watch Philip in action on the polo field. The Queen drove from Windsor Castle in an estate car, but on arrival at the polo ground she changed places at the wheel with Prince Charles. At thirteen, the boy was still a long way short of the age at which teenagers can qualify for the L-test which decides whether or not they can be safely let loose as drivers on what is known as the Queen's highway, but the polo ground at Smith's Lawn, in Windsor Great Park, forms part of the Queen's own property and so is not subject to ordinary legal requirements. Charles slid the estate car smoothly into gear, drove slowly round the polo pitch, with players bowing and policemen saluting, and finally reversed into place to park neatly beside his father's car.

During another polo game at Smith's Lawn later that month, Prince Charles took advantage of the fact that public attention was fixed mainly on his father to change into jodhpurs and sweater and canter off on his own polo pony for some quiet practice.

Between these two weekends at Smith's Lawn came what was literally a flying trip to Germany, in company with his father, to visit some of their German relatives. Through their descent from Queen Victoria and her beloved consort, Prince Albert, both the Queen and her husband have many distant German relatives. Closer still, on Prince Philip's side, are his three surviving sisters, all of whom married German princes. His eldest sister, Princess Margarita, is the widow of Prince Gottfried of Hohenlohe-Langenburg, by whom she had five children. Princess Theodora, a year younger, is the wife of the Margrave of Baden and the mother of four children. Prince Philip's youngest sister, Princess Sophie, has been married twice. Her first husband was Prince

Christopher of Hesse. After he was killed in a war-time air crash she married Prince George of Hanover. She has eight children—five by her first marriage, three by her second.

Only in comparatively recent times have British feelings towards its former enemies of World War II softened sufficiently to permit the Queen to visit Germany and her German relatives. Before that, the most she could hope to do, in a purely personal capacity, was to entertain them quietly from time to time in her own homes. But though, as monarch, she could not herself visit Germany at the time of which we are now writing, this did not prevent Prince Philip making occasional trips there to see his sisters. Nor, on this or other occasions, was there any objection if he wished to take Prince Charles or Princess Anne with him.

There was, at this time, perhaps a special reason for Charles going to Germany with his father. At thirteen, the time was fast approaching when he would leave the preparatory-school atmosphere of Cheam and try his fledgling schoolboy wings in sterner scholastic elements. Charterhouse, Fettes, Milton Abbey, Westminster, Winchester and Trinity College in Perthshire were all suggested as possible schools for the future King by columnists flying kites to see what sort of reaction might be provoked. A small minority, among them Lord Kilbracken, seemed to favour the idea of a state comprehensive school. Eton was, of course, a long-standing favourite and became more so when it was known that Prince Charles had looked round the college during a royal stay at Windsor Castle. It had been, after all, considered a suitable enough choice for his relatives, Prince William and Prince Richard of Gloucester and Prince Michael of Kent. Indeed, as early as the year of his birth, Charles' own name had been provisionally put down for admission to St. Aubyn's House.

But he never went there. As with Cheam, the Queen, readily falling in with the old maxim, 'like father, like son', agreed with her husband that the boy's next step should be Philip's old school, Gordonstoun, in the misty Highlands of Scotland.

Before finally coming to that decision, she had twice visited Gordonstoun, in Philip's company. Charles, too, the person most concerned, went along on one of these visits.

By and large, the Queen's choice, when the news came out, was greeted with approval. "A good choice," observed the *Daily Mail*. "The rather more vigorous disciplines of a school which is in some ways less conventional than others will do the young prince no harm."

Charles was assured of at least one firm friend during the coming first few weeks at Gordonstoun, difficult and strange for him as they were sure to be, his cousin, Guelf, fifteen-year-old son of Prince Philip's sister, Princess Sophie. Charles and Guelf had known each other for years, since they played together as children, barefooted and bare-chested, in the fountain at Balmoral. Now, with Charles' admission to Gordonstoun, Guelf was transferring there from Salem, as Prince Philip had done years before.

Arriving in Germany, Charles and his father stayed first at Wolfsgarten Castle, near Darmstadt, the home of Prince Ludwig of Hesse, a great-grandson of Queen Victoria, and his wife, the former Margaret Geddes. Guelf and his younger brother, George, were also staying there at the time and together the three youngsters, Charles, Guelf and George, explored the extensive grounds of the estate, with its lakes and deer, looked round Darmstadt and drove into Frankfurt to visit the local museum. Charles also went with his father to visit his aunt, Princess Margarita, Philip's eldest sister, whose husband, Prince Gottfried of Hohenlohe-Langenburg, had died the previous year. Father and son stayed overnight with her at Langenburg Castle, near Stuttgart, before returning to London . . . and the switch to Gordonstoun.

III

It was the first day of the 1962 summer term at Gordonstoun, that unusual, rather unorthodox and, in some respects, somewhat Spartan schoolboy establishment on the shores of the Moray Firth. But it was not quite like the first day of any term that had gone before.

A police patrol car was drawn up outside the main entrance to the school grounds. A uniformed constable stood on duty beside it. As each boy arrived for the beginning of the new term, the constable inquired concerning his name and the name of his house, checking the information against a list he held in his hand.

Boys being boys, several of them treated this educational security check as a considerable joke and gave the policeman a succession of false names ... Joe Bloggs, Bill Brown, Tommy Atkins. In vain did the unfortunate constable scan his lists, busily flicking the pages back and forth.

Then, looking up, he spotted sly grins on the faces of the youngsters in front of him.

"Oho," he observed ponderously. "Very funny indeed. And now—what are your *real* names?"

They told him and were allowed to proceed on their way to the school buildings.

The boys at Gordonstoun had known since the term before that their future King was coming to join them in that remote part of Scotland. As a joke, one of them even sent a card for a special record to be played on one of the request programmes from Radio Luxembourg. The record, he wrote, was specially requested for "a certain well-known person coming to join our establishment shortly".

The request was accepted and the recording played on the programme. Its title? *Goodbye Cruel World, I'm Off To Join The Circus.*

Coincidently, as happens almost everywhere royalty goes, the school was somewhat spruced up in readiness for the young Prince's arrival. The road leading from the west gate was levelled and given a fresh coat of tarmacadam. Windmill Lodge, the house in which Charles would be quartered, was given a fresh coat of paint.

Just as he had introduced Charles to Cheam, so Prince Philip now journeyed with him to Gordonstoun and introduced him there.

"That was my room," said father to son, pointing to one of the windows as they went by.

They were greeted by Mr. F. R. G. Chew—known as Bobby to the boys when he was out of earshot. He had been Prince Philip's housemaster in the old days and now, following Dr. Kurt Hahn's retirement, had succeeded him as headmaster. Also in the welcoming party was Captain Iain Tennant, chairman of the school governors, and Mr. Henry Brereton, the warden, and Prince Charles also found himself being introduced to eighteen-year-old Peter Pace, the school's Guardian (head boy), a distinction once held by Prince Philip.

Peter Pace was wearing the school uniform with its traditional open-necked shirt and short trousers. Charles, by contrast, was still wearing the long-trousered suit in which he had arrived. As the party moved from place to place he tended to lag a little behind at times.

"Come along, Charles," his father called briskly at one stage. "Don't walk behind us."

From the granite-built main block of the school, with its turrets reminiscent of a Walt Disney film castle, they drove the quarter of a mile to Windmill Lodge, the long, low building of stone and timber which was to be the young Prince's home-from-home for the next few, all-important years. Here, Charles met his housemaster, Mr. Robert Whitby, a man with a reputation among the boys at Gordonstoun as a fair, firm, efficient disciplinarian, and the head of the house, eighteen-year-old Dugald Mackenzie.

Prince Philip stayed at the school for lunch before climbing back into his car and driving off to Lossiemouth, where his aircraft awaited him. Charles waved his father goodbye and then, as the royal car disappeared out of the school grounds, ran off to change into his new school uniform and to see if he could find his cousin, Guelf, who had arrived at the school earlier in the day by train.

From Lossiemouth, a red Heron of the Queen's Flight took off shortly afterwards with Prince Philip at the controls. He flew low over Gordonstoun, giving his young son a final farewell waggle of his wings before heading out over the North Sea towards Holland where he was due to attend the silver wedding celebrations of Queen Juliana and Prince Bernhardt.

I2   *Gordonstoun*

I

Gordonstoun, where Prince Charles now found himself, has somehow achieved for itself a reputation, enviable or otherwise, as the toughest school in Britain. How far this is true or not, there is no real way of knowing. Some sort of assessment can be obtained by analysing the comments former pupils of Gordonstoun make about their old school, though such comments, inevitably, vary according to the speaker.

Lord Rudolph Russell, son of the Duke of Bedford, for example, has summed the school up in the words: "I was there two years and hated every minute of it. You are always on the go. You get no leisure at all during the day."

By contrast, you have Helene Cordet's son, Max (Prince Philip is his godfather) saying of Gordonstoun: "I loved it. There is simply no comparison between Gordonstoun and any ordinary school. I have been to other schools, both in Britain and France, and they simply don't come up to it. It has so much to offer . . . a tremendous amount of activity, something for every taste, so many benefits, so many facilities, that it is a challenge to take advantage of them. The cold showers, short trousers and morning runs may sound a bit sinister, but you soon get used to them."

And there is no doubt as to what the school's most famous old boy, Prince Philip, feels about his old school. "I thoroughly enjoyed my days at Gordonstoun," he has said.

He retains a considerable nostalgic affection for his old school. When he re-visited it for the official opening of the school's new coastguard station, he slipped away on his own after the opening ceremony and went over to Hopeman Harbour, where, as a boy at Gordonstoun, he spent so many happy hours yarning with the local fishermen and 'messing about in boats'.

At Hopeman he ran into Danny Main, the local harbour-master. "I always like to slip away to the Harbour," he told him. "It brings back so many good memories."

In Prince Philip's day Gordonstoun was in its infancy as a school . . . a small compact community of a comparative handful of boys and a few masters. By the time Prince Charles arrived its boyhood population had swollen considerably. But education there remained decidedly individualistic, with forty-two masters and instructors to 395 boys, a ratio of better than one in ten.

Gordonstoun is picturesquely located among the spruce and pines of Scotland's bleak, windswept east coast, its three hundred acres of grounds sloping down to the sea. It was first founded in 1934 by Dr. Kurt Hahn, with the help of friends in England and Scotland, after he had been forced to flee from Germany as a victim of Nazi oppression. His first scholastic foundation, Salem, on the shores of Lake Constance, which he started under the patronage of Prince Max of Baden, had already achieved considerable distinction both in Germany and beyond. But there was no place for Kurt Hahn or the sort of school he visualised in a Germany dominated by the Nazis. Yet, to Dr. Hahn, it seemed more than ever necessary, in a changing world, that there should be educational establishments designed to counteract what he thought of as "the decay of adventure and enterprise, of skill and care, and of compassion".

In his mind's eye, Dr. Hahn could picture the sort of youngsters he saw as leaders in the future . . . boys trained to exercise independence of judgment and strength of purpose, eager always to protect the weak and safeguard the rights of the under-dog. Above all else, perhaps, boys educated to recognise the true worth of human life.

Prince Philip perhaps had the principles of Gordonstoun in the forefront of his mind when, speaking on one occasion on the subject of education, he defined it thus: "There can be no doubt that all schools have a threefold responsibility of training the intellect, actively developing the character, and providing a practical preparation for life . . . After all, it is the qualities of initiative and perseverance, qualities of the spirit, which are going to make the best use of the trained intellect."

Gordonstoun undoubtedly recognises and accepts this threefold responsibility and its curriculum is aimed not solely at academic learning, but at the healthy development of body, mind and character. The idea has somehow got about that Gordonstoun is dedicated simply and solely to turning boys into very tough young men. This is not the case. Its aims and methods are a good deal more subtle than that. True, it aims at hardening a growing boy while never exposing him to overstrain. But it recognises that different boys have vastly different needs and, based on that recognition, it endeavours to produce resilient bodies to which are coupled trained wills and to stimulate young minds endowed with those reserves of energy which spring from willing and well-conditioned bodies. It by no means regards games, sports and outdoor pursuits as the be-all and end-all of schoolboy life. On the contrary, while recognising the importance of football and hockey, cricket and tennis, swimming and athletics in the development of a growing boy, it keeps such things in their proper place and an outstanding games player is not permitted to become a school hero and the recipient of schoolboy homage, as happens in some other schools both in Britain and elsewhere. At Gordonstoun, schoolboy distinction has to be merited by something more substantial and enduring than a natural aptitude with a bat or a natural eye for a ball.

If the notion that Gordonstoun is dedicated solely to turning out tough young men does not stand examination, neither does another legend which has been woven around the school . . . a legend which the school itself helps to perpetuate in the booklet it sends to the parents of prospective pupils.

"In a plutocratic society," states the handbook, "the Gordonstoun system could not succeed. The law of deterioration cannot be broken unless children born to wealth or position are placed in an environment that frees them from an enervating sense of privilege. This environment can be assured by a sufficient admixture of boys drawn from homes where the conditions of life are not only simple but somewhat hard. Upon such a basis alone can a vital and vigorous school society be maintained."

While it is true that Gordonstoun does admit boys from homes where "the conditions of life are not only simple but somewhat hard", the actual number is small—about fifteen out of a total intake of 395 at the time Prince Charles first went there, hardly sufficient to justify the legend of a completely classless school which has somehow grown up around Gordonstoun. These few scholarship entrants apart (their fees are met from a charitable fund partly subscribed by patrons of the school and partly provided from additional fees paid by the wealthier parents of other youngsters), boys who go to Gordonstoun are mainly the sons of wealthy, aristocratic, land-owning or, at very least, upper middle-class parents.

If Gordonstoun can be said to emphasise one single principle more than any other, it is surely the principle of trust, and, stemming from this, the encouragement for each boy to make special demands upon himself in accordance with the school motto: *Plus est en vous* (loosely translatable as "You have more in you").

"Education," Dr. Hahn said once in a lecture, "has no nobler task than to provide the 'moral equivalent of war' . . . That this task can be fulfilled nobody will doubt who has seen the triumph of mastery in a boy's face when he is conquering adversities on a sailing or mountaineering expedition . . . All boys need the opportunity of proving themselves to themselves, and education must provide such opportunities."

Boys at Gordonstoun are trusted to keep a record of their own marks. This serves as a test of both accuracy and truthfulness. But while Gordonstoun aims at developing trustworthy youngsters, and establishing truthfulness as an ingrained habit, it also allows for the fact that schoolboy consciences should not be too heavily burdened too soon. A system of trust which can be broken with impunity, it argues, is as useless as a system with no trust at all.

So while the boys are trusted, they are by no means trusted blindly . . . at least, not until they have merited trust. Similarly, Gordonstoun has carefully scaled its ladder of promotion and responsibility so that there is no sudden, heady leap from obscurity and subservience to power and privilege. Boys are trained for subsequent responsibility by giving them experience of administration and control in easy doses.

It is usually three terms before a new boy qualifies for his junior training plan. That accomplished, he is, to a large degree, his own supervisor with a sort of gentlemen's agreement operating between him and the school authorities. He must, in short, learn to be responsible for himself before being given responsibility over others. If he errs, it is up to him to record the fact . . . even with the knowledge that such recording may perhaps involve him in punishment. If he is punished, then he must carry out his punishment unsupervised.

Discipline at Gordonstoun is firm and some might even consider it strict. Eating between meals is frowned upon. Smoking is forbidden. Boys are not allowed out after dark. They are not allowed into Elgin, the nearest town, except with good reason and by special permission. Stealing, telling lies, tale-tattling and stupid pranks which involve risks to others . . . these are regarded as the most serious of schoolboy offences.

Seamanship always has been and still is perhaps Gordonstoun's most characteristic activity. All the boys engage in practical seamanship, sailing at Hopeman Harbour in lug cutters, cruising round the Scottish coast in the school's two ketches, *Pinta* and *Soldian*. Mountaineering is another basic and characteristic outlet for the schoolboy spirit of adventure. The school maintains its own mountain rescue unit, its own surf rescue unit, its own fire unit of mobile pumps and tenders (incorporated in the National Fire Service) and its own coastguard station manned by boys trained in the use of life-saving apparatus.

From time to time, all these activities serve an essentially practical purpose. Just previous to Prince Charles going to Gordonstoun, the school fire brigade was called out on one occasion to help fight an outbreak of fire which was sweeping across several hundred acres of Scottish woodland.

There was another occasion when the mountain rescue unit turned out to search for two climbers (not boys from the school) who were missing somewhere in the craggy peaks of the Cairngorms.

A jeep was loaded with climbing ropes, ice axes, blankets, food and first-aid kits and boys of the rescue unit set off into the mountains. Finally they located the missing climbers. They had fallen into a deep crevasse. Members of the rescue unit, along with a stretcher, were lowered into the crevasse to bring them out. One climber, they found when they reached him, was already dead, killed by the fall. The other, badly injured, was rushed to hospital.

The subtle way in which Gordonstoun works on the youngsters who go there is perhaps best seen if one small incident is placed under the microscope. Dr. Hahn, in the days when he was still the school's headmaster, tried to enthuse the boys with the idea of building their own coastguard station to keep watch over the neighbouring stretch of coastline, rocky and dangerous. But the boys themselves were suspicious of the whole business. They felt, as Dr. Hahn put it, that this was perhaps "an enterprise designed for the benefit of their souls" rather than one serving any practical purpose.

Wisely, he did not force the issue. Instead, he asked the Board of Trade to send someone to the school to discuss the project. The Board of Trade not only did so, but offered to meet the cost of installing a telephone if the look-out station was built at a point where they thought it would be of most use.

For a government department to spend money struck the Gordonstoun boys as sufficient assurance that they would be doing something of real value and not simply carrying out an exercise for the benefit of their souls. From that moment, the project went ahead with vigour and enthusiasm.

"It is difficult to sum up our aims and ideals in a few words," Mr. Chew, the school's present headmaster, has said, "but service through self-discipline perhaps comes nearest the mark.

"We aim to turn out good citizens and bring out qualities of leadership in boys who possess them.

"Not all boys are born leaders, of course. So we try not to be a sausage-machine. We encourage each boy to develop his own ideas.

"At Gordonstoun a boy is not judged on his marks in class or his prowess at sport. He is judged by his character development and the curriculum is planned to discover how a boy will behave in the face of discomfort, hardship, danger, mockery and boredom."

It follows that a youngster's final report, when he leaves Gordonstoun for the last time, considers and emphasises two things: his public-spiritedness and his sense of justice.

II

As at Cheam, Prince Charles shared a dormitory with several other boys in his new home at Windmill Lodge. The dormitory floor was of bare, polished wood, and dormitory furnishings were limited to army-type beds and hooks for dressing gowns. But in one respect at least Windmill Lodge was to prove rather more comfortable than Cheam had been. The dormitory was centrally heated.

In accordance with school custom, the royal parents furnished the necessary bed linen, in the shape of sheets, pillow-cases and towels, for their son. Following his experience at Cheam, Charles found no difficulty in making his own bed each morning and cleaning his own shoes. But in some respects, at least, life at Gordonstoun was to prove vastly different from what had gone before at Cheam.

"At Gordonstoun," Max Cordet has said, "the crammed routine is a bit difficult at first and for perhaps the first two months things can seem very strenuous. Then you begin to settle down. I won't say that my first few months at Gordonstoun were unhappy, but they were not easy."

Undoubtedly, the future King found his first few months at his new school no less strenuous than Max Cordet did in his day and it is not unreasonable to picture him turning to 'Granny'—the Queen Mother—for encouragement the weekend she drove to Gordonstoun to collect him and take him back to Birkhall to spend a few hours with her.

One can imagine the Queen Mother, like the wise grandmother she is, assuring her thirteen-year-old grandson that there are times in everyone's life when things do not come easily and that this is especially true of those born to high station.

The school day started at fifteen minutes to seven each morning with a stentorian cry of "Time to get up" from the boy styled 'The Waker' as he made his way from dormitory to dormitory. From then until lights out, nearly fifteen hours later, the school itinerary ran with a clockwork precision which permitted few idle moments.

The Waker's summons was a signal for Charles and the others in his dormitory to tumble out of bed and make their way along the passage to the nearby locker room where dressing gowns and pyjamas were replaced by running shorts and gym shoes. Then it was outside, bare from the waist up, perhaps shivering a little at the freshness of the morning, for a brisk jog-trot along the gravel path or a brief, vigorous session of physical jerks on the Windmill Lodge lawn. Back inside, it was time now for the morning shower—a warm shower for soaping down followed by a cold one, briefly and bracingly, to close the pores and tone up the body. The cold shower also had a further purpose.

"The combination of a morning run and cold shower helps to shake the sleep out of them," Mr. Chew, the headmaster, has explained.

The shower room at Windmill Lodge was equipped with some ten showers to be shared between approximately sixty-four boys, and initially the other boys in the house, perhaps because they were somewhat in awe of this new school-fellow who was also their future King, showed a tendency to move aside so that Prince Charles could take first turn at the nearest available shower. Gradually, however, as they became more accustomed to his presence amongst them, he found himself waiting his turn along with everyone else. But waiting, too, had its uses, he found, as he watched other boys simply turn on the cold shower and run straight through it.

For school work he wore the regulation uniform of dark blue short trousers and a grey-blue open-neck shirt, cotton for summer coolness, flannel for additional warmth in winter. For outdoor wear in cold weather, a naval-type duffle coat provided protection against the elements. Gordonstoun does not favour school caps, blazers or school ties—indeed, ties of any sort—though there is an old boys' tie which Prince Philip nostalgically dons from time to time when he re-visits the scene of so much of his boyhood. One other small idiosyncrasy of Gordonstoun uniform prevented Charles from bulging his pockets with schoolboy odds and bits as he had been inclined to do at Cheam. Apart from a hip pocket in the trousers, the Gordonstoun uniform has no pockets.

While some of the other houses at Gordonstoun had been modernised with a system of electric bells, Windmill Lodge at this time still clung to the old-fashioned handbell and it was the clanging of this at twenty-five minutes past seven each morning which informed Prince Charles that it was time to make his way to the junior common room. Later he was to graduate to sharing a snug, low-ceilinged study, but as a new boy, his periods of private study were carried out under the supervision of a 'Colour Bearer', a senior boy assigned to ensure that juniors worked industriously.

Further clanging of the handbell at eight o'clock was the signal for books to be put away and for each boy to carry out his allotted daily task towards maintaining the cleanliness and tidiness of the school buildings. The common room and dormitories had to be swept, wastepaper baskets emptied, windows polished.

In accordance with his parents' desire that he should be treated like any other boy, Prince Charles carried out each of these tasks in turn. One of his jobs during those early days at Gordonstoun was to help pick up any paper or rubbish littering the yard at Windmill Lodge and, for a time, he was one of a small team of juniors assigned to hump the garbage bins into the roadway in readiness for their twice-weekly collection. But in one respect, at least, he was perhaps fortunate. He found that there was no system of fagging at Gordonstoun as there would have been had he gone to Eton.

Now it was time for breakfast. By this time each morning, Charles had completed his morning run, taken a shower, changed into workaday uniform, done half an hour's private study and his house duty—and it was still only fifteen minutes past eight! As Max Cordet has said, a "crammed routine".

Breakfast was eaten in the main school block, some distance from Windmill Lodge, where a portrait of Prince Philip painted by

Edward Halliday hangs in one of the six dining halls. However, Prince Charles had no occasion to feel that his father's watchful gaze was upon him as he ate. He was in the dining hall above.

As a junior, in those early days at Gordonstoun, the future King, in pursuit of Gordonstoun's policy of training boys to lead through first teaching them to serve, had to take his turn in acting as table waiter, fetching the toast and porridge, collecting the dirty plates and cutlery, and ensuring that the bowls of sugar, syrup and marmalade on the wooden-topped table were always adequately filled. If further supplies were required, as inevitably they were from time to time, he had to race down two flights of stairs to where the housekeeper, Mrs. Sutherland, presided over the hygienically white kitchen which now occupied what had once been the cellars of the original mansion. And the weeks when he did duty as table waiter also found him helping to wipe down the table and sweep the dining room floor at the end of each meal.

At ten minutes past nine it was time for the first class of the day. Each lesson lasted for forty minutes and was followed by a five-minute interval to enable boys to get from one classroom to the next. As class succeeded class, the young Prince found himself occupying a succession of tables each bearing the scarred imprint of the countless youngsters who had sat there before him and in the weeks which followed one table at least was to have the name Charles added to those already etched into its battered surface.

Twice each week, in accordance with Gordonstoun's policy of producing resilient bodies coupled to trained wills, morning lessons were interrupted by the necessity for changing into running shorts and gym shoes for a briefly energetic spell of outdoor exercise. During these morning sessions of physical culture the young Prince ran and jumped, hurled the javelin and threw the discus. If his efforts fell somewhat short of Olympic Games standards, he nevertheless proved himself a more than competent swimmer on visits to the indoor swimming pool in the nearby township of Elgin. With his cousin, Guelf, as his partner, he celebrated his fourteenth birthday by gaining an award for life-saving.

He was no less successful in negotiating the commando course which is among Gordonstoun's more unorthodox features, a test of schoolboy muscle, nerve and agility with its ditch, wall, monkey-net and cat-walks to be tackled in turn before its final awe-inspiring obstacle—a swaying rope suspended above the coldly beckoning water of a small lake. A fall into the lake would have been followed by a purging dose of castor oil in the school's sick-bay. But Charles negotiated the rope safely and this final youthful ordeal was thus avoided.

Like every other boy, Charles was checked in for breakfast, lunch and supper at the dining hall to which he had been allotted. It is a breach of school rules to miss one of the main meals without good reason (though afternoon tea is optional) and perhaps it was a missed meal in the weeks soon after his arrival at Gordonstoun which saw the future King awarded a spell of penalty drill—a uniquely Gordonstoun punishment involving progression round one of the school lawns, alternately walking and running.

Boys will be boys, as the old adage so succinctly expresses it, even if they are also princes. It has been said of Prince Philip's school-days that he was "sometimes naughty, never nasty", and his son would have been less than the real boy his father wanted him to be had there been no occasional transgression of school rules or class-room discipline. One a small suspected breach of classroom dis-cipline resulted in an interview with the headmaster in his study. With any other boy, the matter might well have been dealt with at a more lowly level. But Charles was the future King and some of the masters, no less than some of the boys at Gordonstoun, were at first inclined to react accordingly.

Following his years at Cheam, Charles by now was well ac-customed to the stolid, unexciting fare of school menus and at meal-times he tucked into his food with every sign of schoolboy relish. Lunch on weekdays consisted usually of soup followed by a main course such as stew, fish or cottage pie, with a dessert of rice, prunes or suet pudding to conclude. Roast beef or venison made an appetising change on Sundays. But there was one lunch-time dish which aroused princely suspicions the first time it was set before him.

"Whatever is it?" he asked, dubiously.

"Mooshley," was the reply.

Mooshley (or Musli) is a Gordonstoun speciality which, as Charles doubtless discovered, tastes better than it looks. Served as dessert, it is made from porridge soaked overnight in cream and milk to which sugar, lemon juice, grated lemon rind, grated apple and sliced fruit—bananas, plums or strawberries, according to season—have been added.

As at Cheam, lunch at Gordonstoun, Charles found, was followed by a twenty-minute rest period in the dormitories before buckling down to afternoon activities. Afternoons provided the variety which added spice to schoolboy life. On Monday afternoons there was practical work—P.W. as the boys called it—about the school grounds and the future King was called upon to rake gravel paths, weed flower-beds, push wheel-barrows and generally make himself useful.

Two other afternoons—Tuesdays and Fridays—provided a change of pace. These were the afternoons given over to organised games—cricket, athletics and tennis in summer, hockey and rugby football in winter. Prince Philip, during his time at Gordonstoun, captained both the cricket and hockey teams. His son gave little indication that he might scale similar heights. At cricket, he wielded a fair bat and acquitted himself creditably in the field, but with little sign of real schoolboy enthusiasm. At rugby football, he was briefly energetic in the scrum and was still in his first season when he was selected to play for the Junior Colts against a visiting side from Aberdeen.

After a snowy winter, the pitch was in a sticky condition and it was a decidedly unprincely Prince Charles, face streaked with dirt, clothes and limbs caked with mud, who trotted off the field at the end of the game. He was also considerably bruised, the outcome of some strenuous schoolboy tackling.

There was yet a further change of pace on Wednesday afternoons when Charles, during his first two terms at Gordonstoun, did his pre-Service training, learning to read a map, box the compass, coax a flame from a reluctant primus stove and cook a meal in a mess-tin. He also learned how to treat burns, wounds and fainting and successfully passed a test in elementary first-aid which involved binding the supposedly fractured arm of another boy with splints and bandages.

In battledress and gaiters, an army beret crammed on his tousled head, he paraded with the school's Combined Cadet Force, his uniform immaculately pressed, brasswork gleaming, belt and gaiters scrubbed to pristine whiteness. From a friendly schoolmate he learned that the best way to ensure a really smart turn-out was to rub soap on the inside of the creases before getting to work with a hot iron.

But in all the variety of the Gordonstoun afternoons, perhaps Thursday was the one he most enjoyed. That was the afternoon in each week when he learned the tricks of the potter's craft on the treadle-operated wheel in the school pottery shop. As in the carpentry shop at Cheam, he proved considerably adept with his hands and in July, when his parents paid a flying visit to the school, he was pleased to be able to show them several examples of his handiwork, among them a mug and a jug, a beaker and a vase, a blue and white marmalade pot and an oriental-type head, in the school's arts and crafts exhibition.

Garden work, pottery, rugby football and cadet training are, none of them, exactly conducive to cleanliness and it was perhaps as well that school rules required the taking of another shower, warm and cold, before tea and the classes which followed. Two more classes, each of forty minutes' duration, separated tea from supper. Even then, Gordonstoun's busy day was not yet ended and supper was followed by a further short period of private study in the junior common room.

At half-past eight the clanging of the ancient handbell summoned the boys of Windmill Lodge to evening prayers in the largest of the dormitories. Prayers were succeeded by another brief, but busy, spate of cleaning and tidying up, and by then it was time for juniors like the future King to change into pyjamas and dressing gown in readiness for bed.

In the frenziedly busy life of those early weeks at Gordonstoun, Prince Charles must have found himself, as Max Cordet and others had found before him, with little or no time to call his own. Even his Saturdays were not free. Saturday morning brought classes as usual as well as a rehearsal of the hymns to be sung at Sunday's service; afternoon involved a further hour to be devoted to weeding lawns and raking paths.

But some Saturdays also brought diversion in the form of a film show in the Services Centre. The films at Gordonstoun, Charles found, were rather more adult and certainly more up-to-date than those at Cheam had been and the canvas-backed chair he occupied did nothing to lessen the enjoyment of such epics as *The Bridge on the River Kwai* and *The Guns of Navarone*.

Doubtless he looked forward to the advent of successive Sundays as eagerly as any other boy. It was the one day when he was permitted a little time to himself. There was the luxury of lying abed for an extra hour and a half until fifteen minutes past eight and, usually, the day was his own until it was time for him to sing with the school choir at evening service. But on one Sunday in each term, along with the rest of the boys from Windmill Lodge, he took the mile-long 'silent walk' through the woods—with no talking permitted on the way—to attend morning service at the Michael Kirk, the ancient, granite-built chapel with its weather-worn Celtic cross.

At Gordonstoun, as at Cheam, whenever Prince Charles left the school grounds—as when he went into neighbouring Elgin for life-saving lessons or over to Hopeman Harbour for instruction in seamanship—he was unobtrusively accompanied by his personal detective, at this time a youngish man named Donald Green. The detective had taken up residence at Gordonstoun concurrently with the future King's arrival there, sleeping at Windmill Lodge (though not in the dormitory occupied by the Prince) and eating with the masters in their private dining room.

Prince Charles, by now, was well accustomed to the unobtrusive presence of a detective almost wherever he went. But to his school-fellows at Gordonstoun, the idea of a 'private eye' represented a novel and exciting diversion. Almost inevitably, they tended to make comparisons between Donald Green and James Bond, the tough secret agent of Ian Fleming's thrillers, hotly arguing between themselves concerning the rival merits of the two men, the real-life detective and the fictional secret agent.

Charles apart, the junior boys, in Windmill Lodge at least, became sharply divided into two opposing factions, one section ranged stolidly behind Donald Green, the other supporting the fictional James Bond. Back and forth they argued among themselves, in dormitory and common room, as to which was the strongest, the toughest, the shrewdest, which was the better with a gun and which was the more adept at judo.

Wherever the detective went he was usually accompanied by a small group of hero-worshipping juniors, harrying him with questions. What sort of a gun did he have? Did he prefer a Luger to a Beretta? Had he ever killed anyone?

Adroitly the detective parried their youthful questions with the traditional discretion of those who work for royalty, looking round with feigned furtiveness before lowering his voice to a jesting, conspiratorial whisper.

"I can't tell you that," was his stock answer. "It's a state secret." As an answer it completely satisfied the schoolboy mind while revealing absolutely nothing.

Around the tall, unobtrusive figure of the Prince's detective schoolboy imaginations wove an aura of mystery and high adventure. Donald Green was credited with every talent the schoolboy mind could invent and assigned, in boyish imaginations, to the most outlandish tasks. One story which went the round of classroom and dormitory for a time was that he acted, among other things, as the Prince's food-taster to ensure that he was never poisoned. The story, when it finally reached the ears of Prince Charles, struck him as hilariously funny.

Another schoolboy rumour was that any package addressed to Prince Charles was first handed to Donald Green so that he could submerge it in water before it was opened in case it should contain a bomb.

One day a boy asked Donald Green if the story was true.

"I'm not James Bond, you know," the detective replied, showing that he was not altogether unaware of the schoolboy comparisons which were being made.

By the July, when summer term ended and the holidays began, Prince Charles had begun to find his level in the new, sometimes strange, always busy schoolboy world of Gordonstoun. He flew back to London at the end of the term not in a Heron of the Queen's Flight, but as an ordinary tourist-class passenger aboard an aircraft of British European Airways.

Coffee and biscuits were served during the course of the flight. But the future King, because he was sitting towards the front of the aircraft, was one of the last to be served.

Arriving home at Buckingham Palace, he had good news of his progress at Gordonstoun with which to greet his royal parents. He had started his seamanship classes and had been out rowing and sailing in one of the school's cutters. Only a week before he flew home he had been taught how to handle a canoe, learning to capsize it and, having capsized it, how to right it again. By good behaviour and steady progress in the various branches of school activities, he had qualified to change into the special evening uniform at the end of each day. The right to wear this evening uniform is the first rung of Gordonstoun's ladder of promotion. Academically, according to his headmaster, he was "well up . . . very near the top of his class".

His parents were doubtless well pleased, though Prince Philip, when he was asked how his son was faring at Gordonstoun, replied with one of his customary witticisms.

"At least he hasn't run away yet."

But the remark, joking though it was, surely concealed a father's pleasure and pride in watching his son follow successfully in his own footsteps.

13   *Steady Progress*

I

Charles returned to Gordonstoun in the autumn with a tale of holiday adventure to relate to his friends. His parents, the Queen and Prince Philip, had recently acquired the 63-foot racing yawl, *Bloodhound*, though the acquisition was perhaps more for holiday cruising than for actual racing. With Prince Philip aboard, *Bloodhound* had sailed from Cowes that summer, rounded Land's End and proceeded up the west coast. From Balmoral, where they were vacationing as usual, Charles, not yet fourteen, and Anne, twelve that August, flew to Campbeltown to rendezvous with *Bloodhound*. Carl Gustaf, the young Crown Prince of Sweden, who was staying with the Royal Family at Balmoral, went with them. At Campbeltown, an inflatable dinghy with an outboard motor took them out to scramble aboard *Bloodhound* . . . the start of an exciting and adventurous voyage through Scotland's lochs and canals.

Back at Gordonstoun after the holidays, Prince Charles now had the right to wear what was known as the School Uniform. Of course, he already had a school uniform in the accepted sense of the phrase, but at Gordonstoun the right to wear School Uniform (with capital letters), signified by permission to change into grey-blue short trousers and a light blue sweater at the end of each afternoon, is one that has to be earned. Charles had earned it, and, notwithstanding his unique position as the future King, the fact was celebrated in traditional Gordonstoun fashion.

All unsuspecting, he was quietly changing his clothes in the locker room of Windmill Lodge when he found himself seized bodily by a small group of his schoolfellows. Whooping joyously, they bundled him along the corridor and into the shower room.

Inside the shower room stood a bath of cold water.

169

"In he goes!"

With an exuberant yell, the rest of the group heaved their future King into the bath of water.

"Duck him!"

With another yell, they pushed him under, though only momentarily.

Gasping and spluttering, Charles managed to scramble out of the bath and dashed off in search of a towel.

If the school authorities knew anything of this traditional schoolboy installation, they were careful to turn a diplomatic blind eye to things. To have done otherwise would have meant singling out the young Prince as someone special, which was the last thing his parents would have desired.

Schoolboys are strange young animals with their own strange rites for indicating acceptance (or rejection) of their fellows and this cold-water immersion was one of them, acknowledging the fact that Prince Charles, for all his unique status, had been accepted at Gordonstoun as 'one of the chaps'. To him, at that stage of his upbringing, it was perhaps as acceptable and important a moment of dedication as the ancient ceremony of Coronation which lies ahead of him some time in the future.

He was, without doubt, the world's most famous schoolboy and perhaps—who knows?—at one time in some danger of also being the loneliest. Most of the other boys at Gordonstoun were at first inclined to contemplate him with a mixture of curiosity and awe, and there were many who found it difficult, initially, to treat him as just an ordinary schoolfellow. Their difficulty was understandable. At the back of their schoolboy minds lurked always the knowledge that this was their future King, and overcoming this psychological barrier was not the least of Charles' problems during his first few terms at Gordonstoun.

Not that he was ever entirely without friends. One of his closest friends was his cousin, Prince Guelf. Then there was Lord Brabourne's son, Norton Knatchbull. Another friend was Prince Alexander of Yugoslavia, who had been delegated to show him round when he first arrived at Gordonstoun.

He soon acquired several other, less regal, friends among the boys of Windmill Lodge. In company with three particular friends, he spent many happy, industrious hours renovating an ancient, four-seater bicycle. Working together in the hobbies room, a schoolboy's dream of tools and timber, paint and primers, half-built canoes and dismantled car engines, the four of them over-hauled and repainted their quaint acquisition and were soon speeding round the school grounds on it, pedalling furiously in unison.

There was at one stage during the young Prince's early days at Gordonstoun some degree of irregular traffic in the name-tags used to identify his clothing. Spare tags, embroidered with the name Prince Charles, became something in the nature of desirable souvenirs to be bought and sold or bartered among his school-fellows. It was, of course, nothing to do with Charles himself, and the school authorities, once they were aware of what was going on, took steps to ensure that his spare name-tags were hidden out of harm's way.

As she had done at Cheam, the Queen played her part in ensuring that her son, for all that he was heir to the Throne, had no special privileges to distinguish him from the other boys at Gordonstoun. He was restricted to the same amount of pocket money as any other junior boy and even this he had to hand over to the senior boy in Windmill Lodge who acted as 'Banker', applying for it as it was required.

Like all small boys, there were times when he found himself short of pocket money. One day he went into the small general store in the nearby village of Duffus with the object of replenishing the tuck-box which he kept beneath his table in the junior common room.

The tuck he bought that day came to rather more than he could muster by way of pocket money. Fortunately, his personal detective was close at hand, coming quickly to the rescue with a small, temporary loan.

II

Almost imperceptibly, Gordonstoun's somewhat unorthodox and adventurous curriculum began to harden and toughen the

171

young Prince. Seamanship lessons continued enjoyably. In company with other boys, he went on a number of hill-walking expeditions. For such treks, the customary short trousers were replaced by long ones, for it can be cold and rugged in Scotland's granite-studded hills, and school shoes gave way to stout walking boots. Thick socks, a tartan shirt, a warm sweater and a windproof anorak completed the young Prince's outfit for such expeditions, which sometimes involved spending a night in an isolated hut, with Charles helping to prepare a meal of bacon and beans, toast and coffee, as his father had once done aboard the school schooner.

Friendship with his cousin, Guelf, gave Charles an interest in learning to ski and the following January, after a Christmas spent at Sandringham as usual, he flew out to Munich where Guelf's parents, Prince George of Hanover and Princess Sophie, were waiting to meet him. He was on his way to Tarasp, in Switzerland, with Guelf and his brother George, for a winter sports vacation at the holiday home of Prince Ludwig of Hesse.

In allowing her son to go abroad on holiday, the Queen, doubtless encouraged by Prince Philip, was yet again demonstrating her ability to move with the times. It was a bold experiment, which, unfortunately, did not meet with the full success it undoubtedly deserved. For though the Queen might show herself ready to move with the times, taking the necessary steps to let her children grow up, be educated, come and go as nearly as possible like ordinary youngsters, the rest of the world, as events showed, had not yet adjusted itself to treating them in the same casual fashion.

As a result, what should have been an enjoyable ski-ing holiday at Tarasp was somewhat marred for Prince Charles by the persistent presence of sightseers and photographers, just as an earlier, experimental trip to France had been spoilt for his sister, Princess Anne.

Anne was only eleven when her mother allowed her to make that informal trip, part holiday, part educational, to France. She made the trip as an ordinary passenger on an ordinary cross-Channel steamer. Things were kept as quiet as possible, but, inevitably, the news leaked out, and her stay in France with the eleven-year-old daughter of the Marquis Louis de Saint-Genys was partly spoilt in consequence.

One of the outings planned for the young Princess during that holiday was a visit to Chapelle-sur-Oudon where a village fair was in progress. What should have beeen an enjoyable and informal outing was largely ruined by the crowd of sightseers which pressed round her and the photographers who harried her on all sides. Finally, these goings-on so upset the Princess, bringing her perilously close to tears, that the outing had to be cut short.

Charles' ski-ing holiday in Switzerland was to be similarly marred by public curiosity and photographic enthusiasm. A crowd of some 150 people followed when he ventured out in black stretch trousers and a blue anorak, red and black mittens on his hands and knitted ski-cap on his tousled head, for his first ski-ing lesson. Photographers pounced on him from every conceivable angle at every step. Despite such odds, he struggled through that first lesson with only two spills.

"It was fine," he said, afterwards.

In vain, Princess Margaret of Hesse pleaded with the sight-seers and photographers to leave him alone.

"He has only eight days' holiday and wants to learn to ski and have some fun at it," she said.

But the photographers, at least, took little notice. Some even climbed into the grounds of Prince Ludwig's estate and ploughed stolidly towards the boy through deep snow when he had his daily ski lesson. They were headed off by Prince Ludwig himself and by Superintendent Frank Kelly, Prince Philip's personal detective, who had accompanied Charles on his trip to Switzerland.

That episode so angered Prince Ludwig that he telephoned police headquarters in Berne to lodge a formal complaint. The Swiss police reacted promptly. They announced that any Swiss national caught trespassing on the estate would be arrested, and detailed three men of the local police force to ensure the young Prince's privacy.

After that, Charles continued his ski-ing lessons in the private grounds of the estate under the watchful guard of policemen on skis, a situation neither compatible with the ordinary life his parents wished him to lead nor the most pleasant of boyhood experiences. Nevertheless, by the end of his eight-day holiday he was sufficiently proficient on his skis to pass his first test with a total of twenty-five marks out of a possible twenty-eight.

Returning to Gordonstoun at the start of the new term, he took his skis with him and, on Sundays, he and Guelf, with other schoolboy ski enthusiasts, would board a bus, taking a packed lunch of sandwiches, meat pies, oranges and glucose with them, and journey over to Cairngorm for further practice on the ski slopes there.

The heavy snowfalls Scotland experienced that winter proved ideal for ski-ing practice, but less so for other outdoor pursuits. So thick was the snow at times that even the morning jog-trot had to be abandoned. With weather restricting outdoor exercise, it was arranged for the Gordonstoun boys to go over to the naval air station at Lossiemouth to play handball.

It was from one of these outings to Lossiemouth that Charles was late back . . . a factor which caused schoolboy rumours to start flying thick and fast.

With other boys, he had gone over to Lossiemouth in his detective's Land Rover. Now, with time getting on and no sign of his return, stories began to circulate that there had been an accident.

There is no smoke without fire and the rumours had some foundation in fact. The Land Rover was on its way back from Lossiemouth when it encountered a naval vehicle going in the opposite direction. With the road narrowed by snowdrifts and the surface slippery with ice, the two vehicles skidded into one another. The Land Rover suffered fairly considerable damage, but those in it, including Prince Charles, fortunately escaped with nothing more than bruises and a shaking.

III

Gordonstoun was fast completing what Cheam had already begun . . . turning the child into the boy and the boy into the young man. Already, after only a year at the school, Charles was looking considerably more mature, childhood chubbiness replaced by schoolboy stockiness.

It was an extremely grown-up looking Prince in a charcoal-grey suit who accompanied his parents to Westminster Abbey for the wedding of Princess Alexandra that April, a month which also found him paying a further visit to Pinewood Studios, where he saw part of *Doctor in Distress* being filmed and lunched with the film's stars, Dirk Bogarde, Samantha Eggar and Mylene Demongeot.

His sister, Princess Anne, tall for her age and chief bridesmaid at the wedding, looked equally grown up in a dress of creamy satin, her blonde hair upswept in a mature and fetching chignon.

Both had long since outgrown that period of childhood when they made childishly amusing remarks about the hats and gowns of guests arriving for royal functions and, at the glittering reception and ball given by their mother, the Queen, to mark the coming marriage of her cousin to the Hon. Angus Ogilvy, they were old enough to take their rightful places among the other members of the Royal Family. For both of them, it was their first experience of a royal ball and it seemed somehow fitting that the occasion should prove to be by far the biggest and liveliest function held at Windsor Castle since the far-off days of Queen Victoria.

They both joined in the dancing, Anne partnering the prospective bridegroom on one occasion and Charles dancing with his grandmother, the Queen Mother. Amateur movie-making, as will be judged from his visit to Pinewood Studios, was another hobby which enthused him at this time and he also filmed part of these pre-wedding celebrations from the gallery overlooking the Waterloo Chamber, in which the vast Indian carpet had been rolled back to clear the floor for the dancing.

By that summer, Charles had progressed sufficiently in his seamanship classes at Gordonstoun to qualify for a training cruise aboard the *Pinta,* one of the school's two ketches . . . a cruise which, as events turned out, was to make world headlines.

Each summer, Gordonstoun's two ketches, *Pinta* and *Soldian,* set off, manned by schoolboy crews, for training cruises around the

Scottish coast. At various points of the trip they are met for one schoolboy crew to be taken off and another put aboard. Prince Charles was a member of the crew of *Pinta* when it reached the Isle of Lewis and berthed at Stornoway.

Boys not required for duty aboard ship were allowed into Stornoway, chief town of the islands of the Outer Hebrides, and Prince Charles accordingly went ashore with three of his school-friends and his personal detective.

A Jayne Mansfield film, *It Happened In Athens*, was showing at the local cinema and the detective went along to reserve seats for the party, leaving Charles and the others at the Crown Hotel, where they all planned to eat.

Prince Charles, presumably feeling in need of something to warm the cockles of his young heart, led the way into the cocktail lounge of the hotel, walked straight over to the bar and ordered a glass of cherry brandy. He was perhaps also showing off a little in front of his schoolfellows as youngsters, regal or otherwise, are apt to do. Cherry brandy was a drink he had seen consumed often enough, and perhaps even been permitted to taste, during royal shooting parties. He paid for the drink with half-a-crown and was in the act of sipping it when his detective walked into the cocktail lounge and demanded to know what he was doing.

It was, all things considered, a small enough incident which might well have passed unheeded with any other schoolboy. But Charles was not any other schoolboy. He was, additionally, the future King . . . and perhaps doubly unfortunate in that the whole incident was witnessed by an enterprising journalist with an instinct for a good story.

Even so, the whole business might have blown over much more quickly than it did but for an official denial from Buckingham Palace. Faced with the denial, the journalist stuck by her story. The denial, doubtless due to a misunderstanding of the facts, was subsequently withdrawn and a royal apology substituted.

The outcome of all this was a succession of tall headlines, not only in Britain but around the world.

When Prince Charles first went to Gordonstoun, the headmaster, Mr. Chew, was quoted as saying: "He will be treated like any other boy—and punished if necessary. Definitely there will be no special treatment."

Tackled by the newspapers over the incident of the cherry brandy, he said now that Prince Charles would be suitably dealt with when he returned to school. It was, in consequence, a somewhat glum-looking Prince Charles who emerged from a brief interview in the headmaster's study shortly after his return to Gordonstoun.

By the end of his first year at Gordonstoun, he had qualified for what is known as the Junior Training Plan. Part of Gordonstoun's system of trust is a booklet which a boy is placed upon his honour to complete truthfully each evening. In it he notes down whether or not he has performed certain tasks during the day, whether or not he has broken any of the school rules . . . whether he has dutifully had his two showers, whether he has done his prescribed skips and press-ups, whether he has eaten between meals, wasted time talking when he should have been studying, whether he has given way to any purely personal weakness such as nail-biting.

The right to the Junior Training Plan, as for the Senior Training Plan which follows it, is hard earned and dearly prized at Gordonstoun. And now Prince Charles, as punishment for the incident of the cherry brandy, found his training plan taken away from him.

However, his customary regard for school rules and continued steady progress in various forms of school activity saw it restored to him again shortly afterwards. But some things were less easily mended and there was perhaps additional punishment for the young Prince in the fact that his personal detective, the likeable Donald Green, saw fit to resign his post a short time later.

14   *Teenage Princess*

I

The extent to which Prince Charles had developed and matured during his first year or so at Gordonstoun was never more clearly revealed than during the Royal Family's customary stay at Balmoral in the summer of 1963.

He had been very much of a child still that earlier summer at Balmoral when his mother confided over lunch that she was expecting another baby. Along with Anne, he had run whooping off to the royal nursery to spread the exciting news.

But now, some two months after the episode of the cherry brandy, his fifteenth birthday fast approaching, he was very much the teenage schoolboy in his long-trousered suit when his father suggested a stroll across the Balmoral lawns. The stroll, with Princess Anne included, was to enable Prince Philip to break the news of yet another forthcoming happy event in the Royal Family.

There was, this time, no racing or whooping on the part of Prince Charles. As far as anyone could judge, he took the news of the expected baby stolidly and somewhat phlegmatically, as fourteen-year-old schoolboys are apt to do.

It was left to Princess Anne, nearly two years younger and always the more extrovert of the two youngsters, to display excitement. She turned on her heel, raced back across the lawn, dashed up the granite steps of Balmoral Castle and sought out her mother to confirm this important item of family news.

For Anne, during that summer stay at Balmoral, there was an additional cause for girlhood excitement. She had long wanted to follow in her brother's footsteps by going to boarding school. Now, at last, the decision had been taken and she was to get her wish.

It was midway through September when the Queen interrupted

her relaxing stay at Balmoral and journeyed south to deliver her young daughter safely to her new school at Benenden. A mellow-brick mansion standing at the end of a long drive lined with ancient oaks and chestnuts, Benenden, Anne found, was secluded in its own two hundred acres of grassy parkland, tucked away in the wooded Kentish countryside some fifty miles south-east of London.

Inevitably, the Queen's decision to send her daughter to Benenden brought the school forcibly into the public eye and weekend sightseers became a frequent hazard until the school further concealed itself by the removal of the name-board at the main gates and its replacement with a sign which said simply: Private Grounds and Drive.

Even in Britain, few people had heard of Benenden school until the official announcement that Princess Anne was going there brought it suddenly and unexpectedly into the headlines. Yet for years past it has been a favourite choice of educational establishment for the daughters of parents of position. Princess Benedikte of Denmark was there at one time, and Princess Anne, on arrival, found that she was one of four princesses currently being educated there. The others were Princess Basmah, the young sister of Jordan's King Hussein, and the two small grand-daughters of Haile Selassie, Emperor of Ethiopia, one of whom, Princess Mariasina, proved to be in the same class as the Queen's daughter.

As with many of the boys at Gordonstoun when Prince Charles first arrived there, so it was with the girls at Benenden during the first week or so following Princess Anne's arrival. Initially, at least, she was regarded with some degree of awe by many of the girls who were her new school-fellows, and, despite her delight at going to boarding school, the strangeness of her new surroundings caused her normally extrovert nature to remain temporarily hidden behind an unaccustomed shyness and reserve. But girlhood, like boyhood, was quick to establish its own levels, and just as Haile Selassie's grand-daughter, Mariasina, was merely 'Mary' to the other girls at Benenden, so the Queen's thirteen-year-old daughter was immediately 'Anne' with no nonsense about titles.

Even so, the unaccustomed act of writing her name in the various school books with which she was issued seems to have created a slight problem for her. To have styled herself simply 'Anne' in such books would perhaps have been insufficient. There were doubtless several other Annes of less regal status among the one hundred and nine girls at Benenden at that time. Yet to have defined herself more exactly as 'Princess Anne' would perhaps have been considered somewhat highbrow by her new companions. But even at thirteen the Queen's daughter had already acquired royalty's customary dexterous agility at handling such subtle situations and a satisfactory compromise was achieved with the nomenclature 'P. Anne'.

The Queen's instructions to Benenden's headmistress, Miss Elizabeth Clark, were doubtless as explicit as those she had given at Cheam and Gordonstoun concerning Prince Charles: "Treat my daughter like any other girl." As though to underline her mother's point in this direction, the Princess was already wearing her new school uniform when she first arrived at Benenden. The flat and sensible regulation school shoes perhaps represented no great departure from what she had worn about Buckingham Palace, and while fashion purists may sneer at the traditional old-fashioned navy-blue gym tunic, terminating some inches above the knee, Anne was presumably overjoyed at the opportunity of wearing it. Her long blonde hair had been trimmed somewhat shorter than hitherto to comply with school requirements and the school hat she carried was encircled with the orange band of Guldeford House to which she had been allocated. Her belt and necktie were similarly orange, as was the lining of the long, warm cloak she was to wear for additional comfort during the coming winter.

The Queen, when she took Anne to Benenden, talked briefly with the school's headmistress, Miss Clark, with Anne's house mistress, Miss Cynthia Gee, and with her form mistress, Miss Jean Ormerod. She also took the opportunity of going upstairs to look at her daughter's dormitory, named Magnolia on account of the blossoms which flowered around the diamond-paned window.

"The girls all look so alike in uniform I don't know whether I shall be able to pick out Princess Anne when I come next," the Queen remarked, jestingly, to Miss Clark.

Then, saying goodbye to her daughter, she drove back to London to board a train for her overnight journey back to Balmoral in Scotland. Anne, meantime, was being shown round the school which was to be her new home by another thirteen-year-old, Elizabeth Somershield, one of the three girls sharing her dormitory with her.

Just as her brother had experienced earlier, Anne now found herself faced with the necessity for making her own bed, taking her turn at sweeping the floor and emptying the wastepaper baskets as well as acting as waitress at meal-times. She found herself called upon to wash her own stockings and lingerie and, as the youngest girl in the dormitory, it was also her duty to go along to the linen cupboard each week and collect fresh bed-linen. Not all such tasks, of course, were necessarily foreign to her, but that first weekend at Benenden revealed that she had little knowledge of how to re-make a bed with fresh linen. The other girls in her dormitory obligingly showed her how.

Just as Prince Charles, when he first went to Cheam, had kept a photograph of his pet corgi, Whisky, close at hand to remind him of home, so Anne, now that she was at Benenden, decorated the white-painted chest of drawers beside her bed with photographs of home. There may be a limit to the type of photograph a boy can display without feeling foolish in the eyes of his fellows, but girls have fewer such limitations, and the pictorial display on Anne's bedside chest included photographs of her big brother, Charles, her parents and little Prince Andrew a-straddle a toy horse.

Ever since Charles first went to Cheam, Anne had wanted to go to boarding school, too, confident that she would like it. To her delight, she found herself liking it, as she confided in one of her new school-mates, even more than she had anticipated. She took to most facets of school life as readily as a duck takes to water. There were, of course, one or two small initial complications, like learning to re-make a bed with fresh linen, and at first she found the interval between the first bell at seven o'clock and roll-call, thirty-five minutes later, insufficient time in which to wash and dress, turn back her bedclothes to air and scamper downstairs. But just as Charles had learned that the trick with the cold shower at

Gordonstoun was to turn it on and dash straight through, so Anne, aided by helpful tips from the other girls in her dormitory, soon found it possible to sneak an extra ten minutes of lie-abed luxury on cold mornings and still arrive downstairs, even if a little breathlessly, just in time for roll-call and breakfast.

By Christmas, when she went home for the holidays, her conversation was already liberally sprinkled with strange-sounding words and phrases. She was, her parents learned, studying bilge and stinks among other things—which turned out to be biology and chemistry. She had developed a taste for greased rats, the Benenden nickname for iced buns, available at the mid-morning break. Her description of the school menus included references to bones and barley, which translated into Lancashire hot-pot, Ganges mud (chocolate pudding), frogs' eyes (tapioca pudding) and the horrifically-sounding dead man's leg (baked jam roll). There was also another dessert which it seemed that the girls at Benenden, for some cryptic reason presumably plain to themselves, always referred to as Channel crossing. It proved to be bread and butter pudding.

Like Gordonstoun, Benenden had been selected by the royal parents, in part at least, because it was not concerned solely with either academic success or prowess on the games field. It focuses rather on bringing out individuality, cultivating a sense of humour and developing the ability to see the other person's point of view. Its aims are perhaps best summed up in the words of the headmistress, Miss Clark: "To work hard, play hard and develop each girl's own talents in an unselfish way."

In class, Anne soon proved herself a rather better-than-average pupil and an early report to her parents showed that she was amongst the first five girls in her class of twenty-two. At Latin and French she was soon somewhat ahead of most of her classmates, though, like her brother, Prince Charles, she found it something of a struggle to make real headway at mathematics.

At handicrafts, however, she showed the same real aptitude that her brother had shown in the pottery shop at Gordonstoun, even if, upon occasion, she was perhaps less patient and painstaking with it. She also excelled at dancing, for which she wore a gaily-coloured dirndl skirt, and continued with her piano lessons, practising diligently in the school's soundproof music block.

The compulsory half-hour rest in the dormitory after lunch was followed by outdoor games under the tuition of Miss Alison Cridland, the games mistress. That winter Anne played lacrosse and the following summer she switched to tennis, a game she had previously learned from Dan Maskell, the Wimbledon coach, in lessons on the private court in the gardens at Buckingham Palace. At both lacrosse and tennis she soon showed that she had her father's quick eye for the flight of a ball and she was, in fact, among the first of the new girls that term to complete her initial stick-work at lacrosse.

On afternoons when the weather was too bad for sport, there were long, organised walks instead. On those occasions when the weather was too bad even for walking, team games in the school hall provided an energetic substitute.

With the end of afternoon activities, Anne, in company with all the other girls, would wash, brush her hair and change from her workaday gym tunic into a clean, fresh dress for afternoon tea and the evening lessons which followed until supper at seven o'clock. After supper came prayers in the ancient, panelled school hall with its minstrels' gallery and winding staircase, supposedly haunted by the beautiful, tormented ghost of some unfortunate girl who met an untimely end in the old manor house of Benenden back in the eighteenth century.

School regulations place the 'haunted' staircase out of bounds to the girls at Benenden, and one must await the future memoirs of one of the school's old girls to find out whether the Queen's daughter was ever dared, as most new girls are, to slip out of bed after lights-out and creep up the forbidden staircase, braving a possible encounter with either the ghost or the flesh-and-blood figure of Miss Clark, the headmistress.

As a junior, Anne spent a compulsory quiet half-hour, reading or sewing, each evening following prayers. And three times each week was bath-night when she found herself standing in line with other girls, waiting her turn to take a bath before going to bed at nine o'clock.

On Saturday afternoons she was largely free to follow her own devices. Sometimes, if the weather was fine enough, she would go for a walk, exploring the school grounds and their environs with some of her new-found friends. With permission, it was even possible to stroll into the nearby village with its oak-beamed cottages and quaint, old shops to replenish supplies of such schoolgirl necessities as hair shampoo and candy. For Anne, a favourite purchase was a packet of marshmallows for toasting in front of the fire at night.

II

While Princess Anne was spreading her fledgling schoolgirl wings at Benenden, Prince Charles was forging ahead still at Gordonstoun ... making firm and steady, if unspectacular, progress in class, on the playing field, at seamanship and Gordonstoun's other more unorthodox outdoor pursuits. He was developing schoolboy friendships at various levels, and learning the lessons of lifemanship from the give and take of schoolday environment. Just as he had been meticulously careful when called upon to negotiate the swaying rope above the lake which formed part of the school's commando course, so he was careful always to walk with care along the tricky tightrope dividing the schoolboy from the Prince. Indeed, he was apparently doubly careful following the sea trip to Stornoway and the much-publicised episode of the cherry brandy.

Well aware of the publicity which would inevitably follow if he was caught out in another schoolboy scrape, however innocent, he did not permit himself to become involved on the occasion when some of the more daring spirits in Windmill Lodge staged a night raid on the occupants of a rival house, leaving their victims to awake next morning to find their shoes and towels missing.

He was careful too not to expose himself to criticism through any form of privilege, however small. There was one occasion, on a free Sunday, when he took two of his schoolfriends with him on a visit to his parents at Balmoral Castle. The day passed all too quickly, as it does on such occasions, and when the royal car finally left to take the young Prince and his friends back to Gordonstoun it seemed very probable that they would exceed their ten o'clock deadline.

To Prince Charles' credit, he did not take advantage of his position to have his parents telephone the headmaster and explain what had happened, as, indeed, many boys of no special position might well have done. Instead, he was apparently content to urge the royal chauffeur to faster speed so that he and his friends should not be late. There were, in fact, still about two minutes in hand when the royal car finally deposited the three youngsters back at the school.

But not all his youthful precautions sufficed to prevent a further outbreak of tall headlines around the time of his sixteenth birthday. First puffs of smoke heralding the coming bonfire were some rather cryptic newspaper accounts of a royal essay book reportedly missing at Gordonstoun. Subsequent rumours that the missing book was being offered for sale in London brought Scotland Yard into the picture, and Superintendent Cyril Gold was assigned to investigate what Perry Mason would probably have labelled The Case of the Errant Essays. By this time, as subsequent events were to show, the missing book had already changed hands several times and at a steadily increasing price.

The story that Prince Charles sold the book in the first place to augment his pocket money was later denied by Buckingham Palace. A report entitled *The Princely Pauper* in an American magazine, which also included a suggestion that the young Prince had previously sold his autograph at 'an earlier school', was followed by publication of a letter signed 'Richard Colville, Buckingham Palace'. Commander Richard Colville is the Queen's press secretary.

The letter stated, in part:

"There is no truth whatever in the story that Prince Charles has sold his autograph at any time. There is also no truth whatever in the story that he sold his composition book to a classmate.

"In the first place he is intelligent and old enough to realise how embarrassing this would turn out to be, and second he is only too conscious of the interest of the Press in anything to do with himself and his family.

"The suggestion that his parents keep him so short of money that he has to find other means to raise it is also a complete invention. Finally, the police would not have attempted to regain the composition book unless they were quite satisfied that it had been obtained illegally."

The story, until then, was that Prince Charles had sold the essay book to a school-mate for the sum of thirty shillings. The school-mate, in turn, sold it to one of the school's old boys for £7. It next changed hands when the old boy sold it to a Scottish journalist for £100, showing something over 1,300 per cent profit. In whatever manner the book came into the possession of the schoolboy who sold it for £7, there is little reason to doubt the truth of the subsequent transactions.

From the Scottish journalist the book passed into the hands of a freelance press agency in Lancashire, from where it was recovered by the police, but not before photographic copies had been taken. At this point, the matter became considerably clouded when solicitors acting for the Lancashire agency were stated to have issued a writ against the police claiming the return of the book, and further fogged by the fact that another set of essays—presumably a forgery—was simultaneously being offered for sale around Fleet Street, hub of the newspaper and magazine business, at an asking price of £5,000.

By this time, various foreign publications, scenting a royal scoop, were hot on the trail and the young Prince's essays were eventually to find publication in a number of magazines outside Britain.

It was not the first time the Royal Family had been embarrassed in this fashion. Some years earlier, when Prince Charles was twelve, an American magazine published coloured reproductions of a number of crayon drawings said to be his work, together with a letter in block capitals starting 'Dear Papa' and signed 'Charles' on a sheet of notepaper bearing the royal crest.

Some of the drawings—of a rabbit in a field, a bird on a branch and a sailboat labelled *Coweslip*—revealed not inconsiderable youthful talent. Others, including a drawing of a man in a bow tie captioned 'Papa', a woman in a long yellow gown labelled 'Mumm' and a blue, green and brown van bearing the slogan 'Mr. Charles's Shop', appeared much more childlike in their execution. If they were indeed the work of Prince Charles, they were, like the letter (dated March 25, 1954), executed several years before they were actually published.

Publication of the princely essays in a German magazine brought a comment from Buckingham Palace that the action was 'highly regrettable'. Concerning one of the essays a palace spokesman went further, stating that it was not the original work of Prince Charles at all, but a précis of an extract from *History of England in the Eighteenth Century*, by William Lecky, the nineteenth-century historian and philosopher.

But the other three essays were admittedly the work of the young Prince, and two in particular—entitled *Democracy* and *Press and Radio*—revealed what one newspaper referred to as 'a lively interest in current affairs'.

On the subject of democracy, Prince Charles (allowing for translation into a foreign language and back into English) wrote: "Only if every adult has the right to vote can one say that democracy has been fully realised. Unfortunately the tendency today is to vote for a certain party and not for individual members."

Of radio, television and the press, he wrote that they "protect the people from the Government in many ways by letting them know what is going on, maybe behind their backs in some cases". But he added that the press might do a great deal of harm in the way it criticises various people and thus embarrasses them, and one cannot help feeling that his views in this direction might have been expressed rather more strongly had they been written with precognition as to the ultimate fate of the essay.

The *Desert Island* essay, based on the assumption that a sudden emergency left only ten minutes in which to select four things for life on the island, revealed a sound and practical turn of mind. Prince Charles picked a tent, a knife, some rope and a pocket radio, a selection it would be difficult to better.

It was perhaps no more than was to have been expected that he should have grown several inches during his period at Gordonstoun and at home, on holiday, he was now noticeably taller than his mother, the Queen, though perhaps unlikely to attain his father's more lofty six feet one inch. He had developed in other ways, too. His voice had broken and when the school choir paid a visit to Inverness Cathedral he sang with the basses and baritones.

He continued to play rugby football, but his interest in cricket, for which he had never shown any great enthusiasm, was on the wane and the time was to come when, in place of a spell at the cricket nets, he much preferred a brisk session on the tennis courts.

The toy trumpet with which he had once strutted so proudly along the corridors of Clarence House in childhood had now been replaced by the real thing, and in addition to singing with the school choir, he also played trumpet in the school orchestra during evening service at St. Giles' Cathedral in Edinburgh. More informally, he played the trumpet from time to time with a small beat group which some of the boys at Windmill Lodge formed among themselves, though not all his school-fellows were noticeably enthusiastic about royal attempts to emulate Louis Armstrong. "He drives me mad," one was quoted as saying with reference to the Prince's practice sessions.

By turn, the young Prince had taken part in many different aspects of Gordonstoun's varying activities. He had been on fire-fighting exercises at Lossiemouth naval air station, learned something of the naval arts of signalling and navigation, served with the Sea Cadets, and helped to carry out mock rescue operations with rockets and breeches-buoy as one of Gordonstoun's schoolboy lifeguards. Enthusiasm for pottery continued undiminished and improved techniques brought results good enough to merit the award of a medal at the school's annual projects exhibition.

In class, he proved himself rather above the Gordonstoun average at English and French. His German, too, was coming along well, presumably helped by occasional conversational practice with his cousin, Prince Guelf. He sat for his General Certificate of Education examinations at the 'O' level and was successful in obtaining passes in five subjects—English language, English literature, history, Latin and French. With customary discretion, Buckingham Palace and the Gordonstoun authorities alike declined to reveal whether he had taken any other G.C.E. subjects at which he may have been less successful.

He had, by now, qualified for a study of his own. It was, in fact, little more than a rather large closet in size with a wooden shelf along one wall to serve as both bookshelf and desk. The window of the study overlooked what would be the inner courtyard of Windmill Lodge when work on it was finally completed. The work of constructing this new courtyard was being undertaken by the boys themselves. Just as his father, Prince Philip, had once helped to build a pigsty at Gordonstoun, so Charles changed into dungarees on one afternoon in each week and helped with shovelling sand and mixing cement as the work of constructing the courtyard and its ornamental central pond went forward apace.

In accordance with Gordonstoun's policy of trust, more and more of his school work was undertaken on his own, either in the small private study he now had at Windmill Lodge or in the oak-beamed loft above the school library. Royal princes being little different from other youngsters, there were doubtless occasions when he was guilty of brewing himself coffee or settling down with an exciting novel when he should have been studying. The James Bond books were among his favourite reading at this time.

While his appearance, as he grew towards manhood, may have tended to favour his mother's side of the family, in some respects, at least, the young Prince was taking after his father. He revealed an increasing love of the sea and ships which stemmed from Prince Philip. His interest in polo was another paternal heritage and while on holiday at Windsor he played in a team captained by his father against a team headed by Colonel W. H. Gerard Leigh, chairman of the Household Brigade Polo Club.

There was also some evidence that he had inherited his father's attitude towards photographers, perhaps understandably. There had already been one or two occasions in his young life, notably during his ski-ing holiday in Switzerland some eighteen months earlier, when the attentions of photographers had certainly made things no more enjoyable for him.

Yet it was perhaps schoolboy high spirits rather than actual antipathy which brought about a head-on clash with photographers resulting—initially, at least—in victory for Prince Charles when he flew out to Athens, in company with his father and sister, to attend the wedding of King Constantine of Greece and the eighteen-year-old Princess Anne Marie of Denmark.

Prince Philip was once accused—though recently, in America, he flatly denied the accusation—of playfully drenching two photographers by pressing a button controlling lawn-sprayers at the Chelsea Flower Show. There was, however, no such denial concerning Prince Charles and what happened in Athens.

With other royal guests in Greece for the wedding, he was sunbathing on an offshore raft near the Astir beach club, some twelve miles from Athens, when a party of French photographers headed towards the raft in a paddle boat, cameras clicking as they approached. Charles and Carl Gustaf, the young Crown Prince of Sweden, plunged into the water and swam to head them off.

Prince Charles, according to available accounts, took hold of one side of the paddle boat, while Carl Gustaf took the other. Between them, they succeeded in rocking it so violently that two of the three photographers were projected into the sea along with their cameras and photographic equipment. A third photographer contrived to maintain his balance, but lost his camera in the process.

However, the royal victory was not wholly complete. One of the photographers dived down to retrieve the cameras. The films, undamaged by their immersion in water, were printed and circulated, along with an account of the incident, to make front-page news around the world.

Princess Anne, chief of the bride's five attendants, wore a gown of white organdie trimmed at the hem and sleeves with lily-of-the-valley. As one of the ten crown-bearers, Prince Charles took his turn at holding a jewelled crown over the bridegroom's head. It was a tiring assignment and at one stage of the long ceremony in Athens Cathedral his arm began to sag. The bridegroom's mother, the rather imperious Queen Frederika, promptly stepped forward and gestured to him to raise it higher.

At a ball held in the royal palace, both youngsters, Charles and Anne, looked surprisingly mature, Charles wearing a white jacket with pearl buttons and Anne in a simple sheath dress with a scalloped neckline. By way of additional diversion during this visit to Athens they also toured the ancient ruins of the Acropolis, where Charles made good use of his camera, while the more excitable Anne, gazing out across the Aegean Sea, could not restrain a schoolgirl exclamation of "Isn't it marvellous?"

At Buckingham Palace, the toys and playthings which had once belonged to Charles and Anne had now passed to Prince Andrew, no longer a baby, but already a small, adventurous boy. The nursery schoolroom, too, was now Andrew's province. The new baby, Prince Edward, of course was not yet old enough to share it and to provide Andrew with company during his lessons the Queen arranged for four other small children, two boys and two girls, to visit the palace daily.

Like Charles, Anne had now moved out of the nursery suite into a room of her own at the front of the palace. Once nicknamed the 'Tomboy Princess' by the newspapers, she was growing up tall and elegant, with a graceful sense of movement and developing a considerable dress sense. There was much about her, in appearance and movement, which was reminiscent of her aunt, the tall, statuesque Princess Alexandra. Away from Benenden and free from the restraints of school uniform, she plumped for clothes matching her new-found elegance . . . the simple sheath dress worn in Athens, a light wool suit in creamy checks with a flared skirt and a single-breasted jacket, another in pale grey wool with check pockets and a tie-bow neckline.

Charles, too, was fast emerging as a tall young man rather than a schoolboy, less self-conscious when mingling and conversing with adults than when among boys of his own age. With youngsters of his own age he was still inclined to be a bit shy, at least initially. One girl who danced with him at a private party perhaps came close to the truth about him when she said, "He's only shy to begin with. If nobody stares at him, he comes out of his shell." But about him always there was still that same indefinable air of kingly reserve which had seemed to characterise him even as a baby sitting regally upright in his pram.

III

The Christmas of 1964 brought with it another small but significant break with royal tradition. For decades past the Royal Family had left London each year with unfailing regularity to spend Christmas amid the peace and seclusion of Sandringham. But times were changing and the children were growing up. One can easily imagine with what scant enthusiasm the teenage Charles and Anne viewed the prospect of a long Christmas stay in so remote a spot . . . so far from London with its cinemas and theatres, so far removed from all their youthful contemporaries. One can almost hear, as from teenagers in less regal homes contemplating a similar quiet family gathering, petulant exclamations of "Won't it be dull?" and "What a bore" and "Whatever will we do with ourselves?"

Perhaps imagination stretches the point. The fact remains that Christmas that year, and the following year of 1965, was spent not at Sandringham in accordance with long-standing royal tradition, but at Windsor with advantage taken of the fact to let Charles and Anne have their own teenage dance.

The function was held in what is known as the Crimson Drawing Room, so named on account of its crimson décor and drapes of rich brocade. The royal parents stood with their teenage children to welcome the one hundred and forty guests, mainly young people. But no Christmas party would have been complete without others of the close-knit Royal Family. So 'Granny' and 'Margo' (the Queen Mother and Princess Margaret) were there, too, as were Princess Alexandra and her mother, Princess Marina.

A buffet supper was served and two bars dispensed liquid refreshment, one serving champagne while the other provided soft drinks for those not yet of an age for something stronger. Dancing ranged from Scottish reels through ballroom dances of the traditional type to the latest teenage gyrations, and it may have surprised the royal parents to see how expertly their children performed the Twist with all its latest variations. At Windsor, as elsewhere, the future King, for all his customary reserve and seriousness, revealed himself, in the words of one dancing partner, "a super dancer" and one apparently who knew all the latest 'wiggles'.

193

I5   *The Foothills of Manhood*

I

The future King was now in his seventeenth year. The time was drawing close when he would be ceremonially installed as Prince of Wales and, on his eighteenth birthday, take over in his own right as a member of the Council of State which acts for his mother, the Queen, when she is away from Britain on some state visit or Commonwealth tour.

All this, coupled with the fact that, though still at school, he was a young man rather than a schoolboy, undeniably mature for his years, brought a fast changing attitude among those around him when he was at home at Buckingham Palace. To royal servants, even those who had known him from babyhood through boyhood, he was no longer a child, but a Prince, and one member of the Queen's staff who had long been accustomed to addressing him simply as 'Charles' now found himself taken quietly aside and given a word of advice by one of his superiors.

In future, he was told, he should address the Queen's eldest son by his correct designation: Your Royal Highness.

The time had come, the royal parents decided, when the future monarch might begin to emerge from the cocoon of schooldays and appear from time to time in public life.

Early in 1965, in company with his parents, the young Prince took his place at the state funeral of Sir Winston Churchill and some of those who saw him on that occasion were moved to comment on his growing likeness, in both looks and manner, to his maternal grandfather, the late King George VI. Away from the public gaze, inside Buckingham Palace, Princess Anne, now slightly taller than her mother, helped the Queen to act as hostess to the five monarchs, six other heads of state and sixteen prime ministers who had flown to London to pay their last respects to the great statesman and war leader.

That April, for the first time, Prince Charles was permitted to attend a meeting of the eight-man council which administers the Duchy of Cornwall for him.

The Duchy of Cornwall was created originally back in 1337 by Edward III to provide for the upkeep of his eldest son, the Black Prince. Since then, it has been the inheritance of the eldest son of successive sovereigns. When George II surrendered his other royal lands to the State in return for an annual income—a sound bargain, from the State's point of view, as things turned out—the Duchy of Cornwall was not included. However, in a message to Parliament shortly after her accession to the Throne, the present Queen announced her intention of retaining only part of the Duchy's revenues for Prince Charles during his minority.

A Select Committee was appointed to go into the whole matter of the annuities paid to the Queen (which are known as the Civil List) and to others of the Royal Family. One of the Committee's recommendations was that the Queen should retain one-ninth of the Duchy's net revenues for Prince Charles' maintenance and education up to the age of eighteen, an amount, it was felt, which would also provide him with a moderate capital sum on attaining his majority. The balance of the Duchy's revenues, in accordance with the Queen's own wish, was to go towards the relief of the Civil List.

The Duchy's revenue today derives from some forty acres of valuable industrial and residential land in the London borough of Kennington, and from a further 14,000 acres of agricultural land spread across the counties of Somerset, Dorset, Wiltshire, Devon and Cornwall as well as the Isles of Scilly. Here, it owns farms, villages and tin mines, and, among other things, controls the oyster beds and fishing rights of the Helford River as well as long stretches of foreshore in Devon and Cornwall.

Because it belongs to the Crown, details of the Duchy's revenue are not made public, but Mr. R. A. Butler, the then Chancellor of the Exchequer, moving a resolution in the House of Commons to give effect to the 1952 Select Committee's recommendation, revealed that they totalled approximately £90,000 a year at that time. One-ninth of this gave Prince Charles an income which the Select Committee estimated would produce a total of about £150,000 between 1952 and his eighteenth birthday in 1966. If anything, the actual total is perhaps somewhat larger as the Duchy's revenues have presumably increased as a result of schemes which have made the Kennington acres more valuable by modernising some of the former Georgian and Victorian properties or replacing them with new apartment blocks.

Financially, indeed, Prince Charles' future is amply secure. As long ago as 1952, Parliament also approved an additional income of £30,000 a year for him between his eighteenth and twenty-first birthdays, and it perhaps seems strange, looking back to that time when he was only three years of age, to find that it also decided upon a like sum for his widow in the event that he should marry and then predecease his wife.

But, at sixteen, the young Prince took no part in the business transacted by the Duchy's council, headed by his father, Prince Philip, at that April meeting in 1965. He merely looked on and listened, learning for the future. However, the day was not entirely desk-bound. In heavy rain-showers, Charles and his father later played four chukkas of polo in Windsor Great Park, a form of activity which he doubtless found more exhilarating.

Later that year, as part of his parents' plan for introducing him by easy stages to the threshold of public life, he had a day off from Gordonstoun to attend a garden party for young people at the Palace of Holyrood, the Queen's official residence in Scotland. Standing in line with his parents to welcome the young guests, he displayed, for once, something of his father's informality when one girl shook hands with the Queen and Prince Philip and then continued on her way without seeming to notice the future King.

"Hi, wait a minute," he called after her.

Blushing somewhat, she went back to shake his hand in turn.

In between these two official functions, the meeting of the council of the Duchy of Cornwall and the garden party at the Palace of Holyrood, the young Prince journeyed to the village of

Mersham in Kent on a more personal note. More than sixteen years before, Lady Brabourne, a cousin of Prince Philip, had been one of the godparents at Charles' christening. Now, at sixteen, he could reciprocate by serving as godfather to Lord and Lady Brabourne's twin sons, Nicholas and Timothy. But asked to hold the twins briefly for the benefit of photographers waiting outside the church, he smilingly declined.

While her brother was being gently initiated into various aspects of royal duty, Princess Anne, at Benenden, had realised a long-cherished ambition to go rock-climbing. Dressed in jersey and jeans, anorak and gym shoes, she travelled with other girls to a mountaineering gymnasium at Eridge, some twenty miles away, where, with the girls carefully roped together, she spent a strenuous and exhilarating two hours negotiating a fifty-foot rock-face.

The Queen, on a subsequent visit to Manchester Grammar School, revealed something of a mother's natural concern for her children as they tackle the 'calculated risks' which Prince Philip regards as an essential ingredient for all-round education. She mentioned her daughter's enthusiasm for climbing after watching a climbing display by boys of the Grammar School, adding, "I sometimes wonder if rock-climbing isn't a bit more dangerous than it is made out to be."

Anne's other enthusiasm . . . for horse riding . . . had by now been diverted into more serious channels. There was no longer need for her to gallop bareback round the Balmoral lawns to work off her enthusiasm. Instead, she was allowed to enter for children's competitions, though her name was usually omitted from any official programme to avoid attracting too large crowds and undue publicity.

She had her Irish-bred gelding, High Jinks, with her at Benenden, stabling him at a nearby riding school. But it was on a skewbald named Jester that she was one of the team of four which won the Combined Training Cup on open day. However, High Jinks came into his own at the Badminton horse trials, where, with Charles and her parents looking on, the Princess jumped seven fences to complete a clear round and win a prize of £5.

The passage of years seemed to have eliminated the gap in age between Charles and Anne. Maturing somewhat earlier than her brother, as girls invariably do, Anne now seemed on a par with Charles, despite his twenty-one months' seniority, whenever the two of them were together. Schooldays separated them, of course, but on holiday they were still frequently together, still closely companionable.

They were together at the Game Fair at Shotover Park in Oxfordshire, where Charles, in particular, watched with an experienced eye as one of the royal labradors, Sandringham Ranger, took part in the gun-dog tests. They were together aboard *Bloodhound* for the racing at Cowes, with Anne wearing what observers variously described as a Bob Dylan or a Beatle-type cap. When Charles played polo at Smith's Lawn, Anne was there to hold his pony for him and lead it away at the end of a chukka. Despite some tactical advice from his father, Prince Philip, Charles was unable to prevent his team, Rangers, losing one game by five goals to three, though they acquitted themselves more creditably the following day in achieving a seven-six victory.

While there may have been few indications during his years at Gordonstoun that Prince Charles would ever surpass his father's achievements on the sports field, in another direction at least he revealed quite considerable and perhaps hitherto unsuspected talent. This was in the field of drama. In a school production of Shakespeare's *Henry V*, with smaller boys whose voices had not yet broken handling the lighter, feminine roles, the future King was given the part of the Duke of Exeter. So well did he acquit himself that he established a reputation as 'one of the best actors in the school'. It was as though on stage, acting a part, he could somehow shed, however briefly, the regal reserve and inhibitions which, though less marked than formerly, were still there in schoolday life.

One consequence of his fine performance in *Henry V* was the title role in a subsequent production of *Macbeth* . . . and again he acquitted himself with considerable distinction. His royal parents, the Queen and Prince Philip, travelled by overnight train from London to Scotland to see the play as members of an invited audience of some one hundred and fifty people. Though they were perhaps too modest to say so, doubtless they echoed the opinion of Mr. Chew, Gordonstoun's headmaster, that their son, who had celebrated his seventeenth birthday some two weeks previously, handled the difficult and demanding role of Macbeth 'excellently'.

For Prince Philip, that overnight trip to re-visit his old school in Scotland was also by way of being a sentimental journey. Watching his son, handsomely bearded in the role of Macbeth, Prince Philip's mind must surely have gone back over the years to the days when he was a boy at Gordonstoun and had acted the comparatively minor part of Donalbain in that selfsame play.

The beard Prince Charles wore for the production was not his own, but an exceptionally well-devised piece of theatrical make-up. However, he wore no wig. "His own hair was long enough," Mr. Eric Anderson, the master who produced the play, was quoted as saying ... a remark carrying slight echoes of those earlier years when the young Prince's tousled hair-style had sometimes brought newspaper columnists to the verge of apoplexy.

When Prince Charles arrived home for the Christmas holidays in December, 1965, he had another exceptionally pleasing item of news for his royal parents. He had won a silver medal in the youth project which bears his father's name ... the Duke of Edinburgh's Award Scheme.

Pioneered by Prince Philip in 1956 to help in the character training of the young, not only in Britain but throughout the Commonwealth, the award scheme is designed in four parts—rescue and public service, expeditions, pursuits and physical fitness—with certificates, badges and medals for those who attain the appropriate standards. Charles' silver medal had followed his training in first-aid, improved skill at pottery, an expedition in the Cairngorms and ability at athletics. It was presented to him, prior to his return home, by Gordonstoun's headmaster, Mr. Chew. Still in the future was the possibility of a gold medal which, for other youngsters, includes the honour of an invitation to Buckingham Palace for the medal to be personally presented by Prince Philip himself. For Prince Charles, entry into Buckingham Palace may be no novelty, but no one can doubt that whatever witty asides might pass between them, such an occasion would be a source of immense pride and pleasure for father and son alike·

Prince Charles, when he returned home to Buckingham Palace that December, was bidding a longer-than-usual farewell to Gordonstoun. It would be many months before he next saw its granite walls and was reunited with his friends in Windmill Lodge . . . and the period between would have seen him travelling half across the world.

The decision concerning that part of his future education had already been taken by his royal parents. But with his eighteenth birthday now less than twelve months away, other decisions necessary to fit him for his future high station in life could not be long delayed nor decided on so personal a family basis. The years of manhood which lay ahead belonged not to him and his family alone, but to Britain at large and indeed the whole Commonwealth of Nations. The time had come for other high authorities to be consulted about the future.

Accordingly, State and Church, the Universities and the Armed Services were alike represented at a small dinner party held at Buckingham Palace shortly after the young Prince arrived home from Gordonstoun that Christmas. The four guests who joined the Queen and Prince Philip for dinner that night were the Prime Minister, Mr. Harold Wilson, the Archbishop of Canterbury, Dr. Michael Ramsey, Prince Philip's uncle, Admiral of the Fleet Earl Mountbatten of Burma, and Professor Sir Charles Wilson, the chairman of the Vice-Chancellors of Universities committee. The main subject of discussion during and after dinner was the future education and further training of the young man destined to be the future King.

II

One outcome of the Queen's state visit to Germany early in 1965 was a rumour that the young Prince of Wales might soon be transferring from Gordonstoun to Salem. Another story around this time was that he might continue his education at Atlantic College on the coast of Wales. In fact, his royal parents had something else in mind.

The Queen, during her last tour of Australia, had promised Australians that she would "send my eldest son to visit you, too, when he is older". Most people had taken this to mean that the future King, once his schooldays were over, would find himself embarking on a succession of visits to the countries of the Commonwealth, just as the Duke of Windsor did in the days when he was Prince of Wales. But as things turned out, the Queen's promise to Australia was to be fulfilled much more quickly than that, and October of 1965 brought the surprise news that Prince Charles was to spend a term at school in Australia on an exchange basis with an Australian youngster of around the same age. The school selected to give the future King his first small view of life in a Commonwealth country was the Geelong Church of England Grammar School, though Prince Charles went not to the main school at Corio, thirty-seven miles from Melbourne, but to Timbertop, the middle school set on the lower slopes of the Great Dividing Range.

The idea of sending their son to school for a time in one of the main countries of the Commonwealth emanated entirely with the royal parents. But once the decision was taken in principle, they consulted with Australia's Prime Minister, Sir Robert Menzies, when he visited them at Balmoral during the summer, and also with Mr. Thomas Garnett, Geelong's headmaster, who was coincidently touring Britain at that time.

Prince Charles, himself, according to a Buckingham Palace spokesman, was "involved in the plan from the beginning and he is very happy at the prospect", a fact which Mr. Garnett was happy to confirm. "I have talked to the Prince," he said, "and he is looking forward to coming as much as we are looking forward to having him." Gordonstoun's headmaster, Mr. Chew, saw the schoolboy Prince as "an excellent ambassador in every way".

For cartoonists and comedians, the news provided an opportunity for humour. One newspaper published a cleverly contrived photograph showing what Prince Charles would look like in an Australian bush hat. The Royal Variety Show, which the Queen and Prince Philip attended a few weeks later, included a comic sketch purporting to show the staff at Timbertop eagerly awaiting the arrival of the new pupil.

But not everyone took the news in the same lighthearted vein. While most people in Britain approved the idea, one newspaper columnist was moved to query whether the heir to the Throne was "genuinely enjoying a more contemporary education than Queen Victoria's heir, later King Edward VII" and went on to comment: "A modern education is no longer built on the theory that 'toughness' moulds the character. Psychology has changed our views. Besides, the cold bath, the iron bedstead and the rigours of the lumber camp are not very relevant to the modern world."

Such criticism was not occasioned by the fact that Prince Charles was going to Australia, but by the type of school to which he was going.

Situated 2,000 feet above sea level in wild, rough country, some 116 miles north-east of Melbourne, picturesquely located amidst blue rocks and tall gum trees, Timbertop was the original brain-child of Dr. J. R. Darling, a former headmaster of Geelong Grammar School and subsequently chairman of the Australian Broadcasting Commission. His idea was to give boys of the middle school some firsthand experience of what it was like to live in the bush ... that same concept of rugged upbringing which causes Gordonstoun to include hill-walking, rock-climbing and similar adventurous activities in its educational syllabus.

About one hundred and thirty-five Geelong boys go to Timbertop at any one time. While there, they live a rugged, backwoods-type life, sleeping in timber-built chalets, wearing what they like—"we encourage them to wear out their old clothes"—and following a concentrated curriculum which includes wood-chopping, chicken-raising, pig-breeding, gardening, fishing and climbing as well as more orthodox academic studies.

Prince Charles, when he went there in February, 1966, was already seventeen, which made him senior to most of the other boys at Timbertop. But the taste of Australian life which he found himself sampling was very much a new experience, totally unlike anything which had gone before. While the comparative ruggedness of life in the bush may not have disconcerted him—"We're supposed to be pretty tough here, too, you know," his headmaster at Gordonstoun had commented in advance—he doubtless found, as his parents had found before him, that Australians have few inhibitions in their attitude towards royalty and that, prince or no prince, a 'pommie' is still a 'pommie'.

If there were those in Britain who visualised the Prince's new school as a sort of educational 'lumber camp', there were those in Australia who saw it as precisely the opposite—as a sort of antipodean Eton College. This fact was made abundantly plain in Australia's House of Representatives, prior to the future King's arrival, when a Labour member queried the royal parents' decision to send their son to what is "generally accepted as the most exclusive school in Australia".

Its exclusivity may not have been of paramount importance to the royal parents in their choice of school, but, as in the case of Cheam and Gordonstoun, location and isolation presumably were.

As Sir Robert Menzies explained to the House of Representatives: "Geelong Grammar is a school of high repute and it is not difficult for people to understand that a school that has a rural branch has attractions in this instance.

"I would be very sorry for the young Prince if he were at school in the middle of a crowded city in Australia with people gazing at him, people trying to get pictures of him and with people making him a raree-show."

While the original royal plan was for Prince Charles to spend only a single school term in Australia, the possibility that this might be extended once he got there was clearly foreshadowed when, packing for the flight out at the tail-end of January, he decided to include his skis. For reasons best known to himself, however, he left his trumpet behind.

His father and sister, very much a young lady at fifteen, accompanied him to London Airport to see him off. The Queen confined her goodbyes to the privacy of Buckingham Palace.

Facially, Charles may take more after his mother's side of the family, but as the two of them, Prince Philip and Prince Charles, walked together to the waiting aircraft there could be no mistaking that they were father and son. They walked with matching strides, both hatless and coatless, both with their left hands thrust casually into their jacket pockets. Even the handkerchiefs peeping from their breast pockets were squared off in identical fashion.

Prior to his departure for Timbertop, Prince Charles had been guest-of-honour at an informal luncheon party given by Sir Alexander Downer, the Australian High Commissioner in London. While other guests sipped their sherry or martinis, the young Prince contented himself with a pre-lunch tomato juice and equally declined a cigarette which was offered to him. On the other side of the world, in Canberra, newspapermen were being briefed that he was rather "a shy young man" who might well retreat into his shell if they bothered him over-much, but at that luncheon party in London he revealed himself an easy conversationalist with a lively sense of humour.

He joked at suggestions that he might find himself doing duty as a "slushy" at Timbertop, serving meals and helping with the washing-up (a task in fact confined to the younger boys), and smilingly doubted that he would be chopping much wood. With the cherry brandy episode on Stornaway apparently still in mind, he also made a joke about the nearest pub to his new school in Australia and, curiously, seemed to know its exact location . . . in the small village of Merrijig, three miles from Timbertop.

At the same time, he was clearly eager to find out all he could about the new way of life which lay briefly ahead of him in Australia. "Tell me, what is Timbertop really like?" he asked a fellow-guest who had himself been a youngster there not so very many years before.

The flight out, in a Qantas Boeing 707, was by way of New York, San Francisco, where he gave a lively and unscheduled press conference, and Honolulu, where an uninhibited teenage American girl with the somewhat improbable name of Star Fluke garlanded him with the traditional Hawaiian *lei* and planted a spanking kiss upon his cheek.

An earlier attempt at garlanding him as he walked from his aircraft to the V.I.P. lounge on arrival at Honolulu had been less successful. "Ha, you missed," he called out triumphantly as the floral *lei* fell a few feet from him.

But Miss Fluke's subsequent successful attempt took him by

surprise and, somewhat startled, he could only gasp a smiling, "Oh, thank you."

The less inhibited Miss Fluke confided later that, to her, the act of kissing Britain's future King was "like a dream come true". It was, after all, a perfectly harmless, spur-of-the-moment spot of teenage fun which amused even the Queen when she heard of it.

"Well, he is growing up, isn't he?" she remarked, laughingly.

The flight was a routine one with ninety-nine other passengers aboard the aircraft for the final leg of the journey. There were in fact some seventeen other passengers in the first-class compartment where Prince Charles sat beside his equerry, Squadron Leader David Checketts. Immediately behind sat Detective Inspector Derek Sharp, the Australian police officer assigned to watch over him during his spell at Timbertop.

For part of the trip, Charles relaxed in a pullover of pale grey lambswool, but just before the aircraft touched down in Sydney he replaced the pullover with the jacket of his dark grey suit. Prince or no Prince, he was required to comply with the usual customs and immigration formalities, and the printed form which air hostess Janette Shannon handed him towards the end of the long haul from London to Sydney demanded assurance, among other things, that he was carrying no "spring-backed knives, daggers, coshes, knuckledusters, swordsticks, narcotics, insects, bulbs or sausage-meat".

Cries of "Good on you, Charlie" greeted him as he emerged from the aircraft in his dark grey suit with its matching tie and blue shirt, hands clasped behind his back in the familiar royal pose, and Australia's first impression of the future King was perhaps pinpointed by the man in the crowd who exclaimed involuntarily, "Isn't he like his father?"

From Sydney he flew on to Canberra where, skipping lunch, he went straight to bed at Government House to catch up on lost sleep. But by evening, when he dined with the Governor-General and Lady Casey, he was chatty and smiling again.

Three relaxing days were spent in Canberra before continuing the journey to Timbertop. During that time, Charles went horseback riding over the undulating hills of a nearby sheep station, sailed on Lake Burley Griffin in the company of twenty-five-year-old Leonie Tyrrell, daughter of the official secretary to the Governor-General, and took a close look at the kangaroos and wallabies in the 250-acre Gungahlin wildlife reserve, where the sight of a baby kangaroo in its mother's pouch brought the royal camera into immediate action.

Two more stages of his long journey yet remained . . . a flight to Mangalore and a car trip from there to Timbertop. At Mangalore, in striking contrast to the wet and wintry weather he had left behind in London, the temperature stood at 80 degrees (Fahrenheit). A reddened royal face already showed signs of over-exposure to the hot Australian sun. But the Prince was in high fettle, exchanging shouted pleasantries with one woman in the small crowd waiting to greet him.

"I hope you don't get sunburnt," he called out to her in a manner reminiscent of his father's offbeat approach to such royal occasions.

"I won't—and I hope you don't," she called back. "I'm used to it."

"I'm afraid I'm not," Charles replied, and his rueful grin matched the redness of his face as he climbed into the waiting car which was to take him on the last seventy-eight miles of his journey.

At Mansfield, the nearest shopping centre to Timbertop, practically the whole of the town's 2,000 population had turned out in the hope of seeing him. "Prince Charles and decimals all at the same time—I don't know how we'll cope," one resident quipped.

Fourteen miles from Mansfield the royal car turned off on to a dirt road in the direction of a fingerpost pointing to "Timbertop." Two miles further along the dirt road it came to a gate and a sign which said uncompromisingly, "Stop. Private Property." Prince Charles had arrived at his destination.

His first glimpse of his new school revealed clearly that Timbertop was aptly named, a collection of timber-built chalets and schoolrooms, cooking and dining quarters, assembly hall and a contemporary-looking, triangular-shaped chapel scattered about a bushland hilltop in landscape as rugged and picturesque as even Australia can boast. He counted nine residential chalets, each with its own living room, dormitory and kitchen, on his first quick inspection. Each chalet, he found, housed fifteen boys who slept on divan-type beds beneath which were drawers for their clothes and belongings.

But Charles, with the other senior boys, found himself with his own sitting-room which was to serve also as a study. It was a room with a handsome brick fireplace and a floor-length window looking out on to the wide panorama of bushland and mountain. Bookshelves, easy chairs and a hard-backed chair at a stout wooden table completed the furnishings. The meal which greeted his arrival was a thoughtful blending of the old and the new. Britain's traditional roast beef and Yorkshire pudding was followed by Australian pineapple and rock melon. Charles tucked into it with every sign of relish.

Subsequently he was taken on a conducted tour of his new surroundings. He was shown one of the large, smelly, narrow-necked bottles employed to entice and trap the abundant flies which infest the area, was very nearly kicked in the face by an over-enthusiastic youngster demonstrating the knack of rope-swinging, and experimented briefly with the fire-fighting gear which is a necessary part of the school equipment in that remote and heavily wooded spot. Perhaps mindful of the accusations which attached themselves to his father after a visit to the Chelsea Flower Show, he uttered a cautionary "Watch your feet" before trying his hand with a portable fire-spray.

With photographers and newspapermen looking on, two strapping fifteen-year-olds showed him how to slice through a red gum log with a bushman's saw. The saw was passed to Charles and Stuart McGregor, another seventeen-year-old, for them to display their prowess. The two fifteen-year-olds, doubtless going all out to display their ability, had taken a mere eight seconds to slice through the three-inch log. Charles and his partner took rather longer—twenty-one seconds—though part of the difference was due to deliberately slowing down at one stage for the benefit of the photographers.

Then the reporters and photographers took their leave and the future King, more secure from public gaze at Timbertop than he had been even at Gordonstoun, could settle again to the task of equipping himself for manhood and future monarchy. He was up before half-past seven for breakfast the following morning. He attended prayers in the school's triangular-shaped chapel and, as a senior, spent much of the remainder of the day supervising the uncrating of books and handing them out to the one hundred and thirty-five junior boys.

Neither that day nor in the weeks which followed was he treated like an ordinary schoolboy. For one thing, he was two years beyond the average Timbertop age of fourteen to fifteen and his studies were that much more advanced. For another thing, he was the future King, his royal status underlined by the "hot line" which now linked Timbertop with Melbourne and Canberra and thence with London should the occasion require it.

To ease him into his new and undeniably strange surroundings he had the company of two other young men of around his own age, Stuart McGregor, a sheep farmer's son from Victoria who had been captain of school football the previous year, and John Burnell, previously the head of school. They shared the study in which Charles was given special tuition towards his G.C.E. 'A' levels in French, English and history and where, between spells of tuition, he studied on his own with the aid of books brought with him from London.

For meals, he sat at a table with the "leaders" (roughly equivalent to the Colour Bearers at Gordonstoun and the prefects at more orthodox schools) in the main dining hall, eating food served on unbreakable plastic plates. After school each day he helped to supervise the younger boys as they toiled at cutting wood, emptying the messy fly-traps, burning food scraps and generally tidying the school surrounds.

All the time, of course, the accent was on the great outdoors. During his first week at Timbertop Charles swam in the school dam, joined in the weekly cross-country run and went on a bush-land trek designed to teach the rudiments of pitching a tent, lighting a fire and, most important of all in those surroundings,

209

fighting a bush fire. For horse-riding, arrangements had been made for him to borrow a mount from a neighbouring establishment run by an Australian show-jumping champion, and he was also issued with a licence to go fly-fishing on the Howqua River, where at least one local resident has contrived a novel method of fishing from horseback. Weekends brought the traditional Timbertop toughening-up experience of a long trek through the bush with bedding, tucker and anti-snakebite kit.

Except in its detail, it was, on the face of it, a way of life not so very different from what he had known at Gordonstoun. But there were, below the surface, certain other differences which would presumably exert their influence, given time. As Geelong's headmaster pointed out: "People keep saying Timbertop is like Gordonstoun, but the two schools couldn't be more different. Gordonstoun has boys of all ages, while here they are all of one age group. Here, the boys are in much smaller groups, which is important. And here there are no formal games."

As a change of pace one week, Prince Charles, accompanied by Stuart McGregor, drove over to Shepparton, some sixty miles away, to see an exhibition of paintings by the Australian artist, Sidney Nolan. So unobtrusive was his visit that he had come and gone before either the town's mayor or even the local police chief knew that he had been there.

While Charles was adjusting himself to the new, strange life of Timbertop, his exchange student, David Manton, the son of a sheep farmer, was proving his worth at Gordonstoun. Tape recordings arriving in place of letters at his parents' home in Riddell's Creek, Victoria, informed them that he had gained his athletic colours soon after arriving at Gordonstoun, and in one cross-country run, with boys from all over Scotland taking part, he was the first Gordonstoun runner home.

The end of his first term at Timbertop brought Prince Charles a happy reunion with "Granny"—the Queen Mother. The Queen Mother, seemingly as indefatigable as ever in her sixty-sixth year, was making an extended tour of Australia and New Zealand to compensate for the one she should have made the previous year and which she had to cancel when she was hurried to hospital for an appendicectomy. Grandson and grandmother arranged to meet in Canberra and on the way there from Timbertop Charles stopped off briefly at Coldstream, near Melbourne, for an impromptu game of polo with members of the Yarra Glen-Lilydale Club.

Playing three to a side (instead of the usual four), Charles skippered his team to victory, scoring two of the goals himself. Club president John Lithgow, who also took part in the game, commented afterwards, "Prince Charles is an extremely good horseman and has a keen eye when it comes to hitting the ball. Given another couple of years, he will be a jolly good player." It was a comment which must surely have delighted the polo-playing heart of the boy's father.

At Canberra the brief reunion between grandson and grandmother was marked by an affectionate hug and kiss on both sides. Together, the two of them attended the parish church of St. John the Baptist in Canberra and dined with the Prime Minister and Mrs. Holt before the Queen Mother set off on her subsequent tour of the Snowy Mountains. Prince Charles accompanied her. It was his first experience of a royal tour, another landmark along the road to monarchy, and was highlighted by a near-accident. A honeymoon couple coming the opposite way were seemingly so excited at the prospect of seeing the Queen Mother that they nearly collided with her accompanying police car. The royal Rolls Royce was forced to swerve as a result, but was otherwise uninvolved. "No real risk," the driver of the Rolls commented laconically.

For Prince Charles that brief reunion with the grandmother to whom he is so closely attached was in very different terms to the one which took place shortly after he first went to Gordonstoun. Then he had asked her if it was possible to leave his new school. But now, in Australia, he was keen to stay on.

From Canberra, where he said goodbye to his grandmother at the end of their trip together, he also put through a telephone call to his parents at Buckingham Palace. Immediately following that telephone call came the official announcement that he would be staying on in Australia for a second term, a period during which the forethought of packing his ski equipment would presumably stand him in good stead.

III

Prince Charles returned home with his face bronzed by the Australian sun and his horizons doubtless broadened by the time spent among Australia's uninhibited youth. Ahead of him lay not only further academic learning but also the prospect of a gradually increasing number of away-from-school royal duties to help equip him for the years of princely life and subsequent monarchy which lie ahead of him.

His future was ordained at birth and his life moves steadily towards fruition along its destined path. It is a prospect which neither disturbs nor excites him. Like his mother, the Queen, he sees it as his required duty, a task to be tackled as thoroughly and conscientiously as possible.

What lies ahead of him when his schooldays are finally over . . . will his role as heir to the Throne be as unorthodox, by royal standards, as his education has been?

It seems unlikely. Well-intentioned suggestions that he may perhaps carve a career for himself right outside the royal round—in commerce or industry—would hardly seem to be rooted in reality. Even if this were his wish, royal duty would doubtless decree otherwise.

Never in history have there been so many demands for the presence and patronage of the Royal Family as there are today. They come not only from all parts of Britain, but equally from the countries of the Commonwealth, and, indeed, from countries unconnected, other than in friendship, with either Britain or the Commonwealth.

That the Queen and Prince Philip accede to as many such requests as possible is clearly apparent. But even the seemingly indefatigable Prince Philip, carrying out perhaps three or four public engagements to each one fulfilled by the Queen, hedge-hopping by helicopter from one part of Britain to another, jet-flying to all parts of the world, can still accommodate only a percentage of the requests and invitations so constantly showered upon him.

Others of the Royal Family help out, of course. The Queen Mother, the Duke of Gloucester and Princess Marina shoulder a share of the burden. The Queen Mother, indeed, shoulders perhaps more than her share. Princess Margaret and Princess Alexandra assist too. But on the male side there seems a disinclination among the younger members of the family to tackle the traditional chores of the royal round. The Duke of Kent and his brother, Prince Michael, seem bent on their military careers. Prince William of Gloucester, too, has shown that he prefers a working role outside royal life.

With the Queen Mother, Princess Marina and the Duke of Gloucester getting no younger, someone else is needed. The young Prince of Wales, as he approaches manhood, is the obvious someone.

Of course, nothing can be taken completely for granted in a day and age when royalty has shown that it is capable of changing its traditional pattern of life along with everyone else. Yet the future King's immediate destiny would seem clear. As he awaits the high office of monarchy, he will, like his mother before him and her father before that, shoulder an increasing share of the public duties which are royalty's main function.

For him, the ceremony of Coronation to which he has been born may lie far in the future. His mother, it is true, became Queen at the youthful age of twenty-five, his grandfather, King George VI, having died at the comparatively early age of fifty-six.

But his great-grandfather, King George V, reigned for a quarter of a century and was seventy when he died. His great-great-grandfather, King Edward VII, son of Queen Victoria, was a man nearing sixty when he ascended the Throne. Queen Victoria, in fact, lived to the ripe age of eighty-one and was on the Throne for sixty-three years.

So Prince Charles could be a man in middle age before he succeeds to the Throne.

What sort of king will he be? How far is it likely that he will change the face of monarchy?

Prophecy in such things is always dangerous, but the broadening of outlook brought about by school life could be reflected, when the time comes, by a broadening of the court circle so that the atmosphere around the Throne, less rarified now than a generation ago, becomes less rarified still. Even before that, his obvious interest in creative things, in drama, music and pottery, developed during his school years, could see in him a new royal patron to give a resurgence to the arts.

One more intriguing riddle remains to be answered. When Charles is King, who will be Britain's queen? Today, as the future monarch ascends the foothills of manhood, the question has considerably more point to it than it had when he was a mere boy.

The final answer still lies hidden in the mists of the future, but it is possible to propound a proposition or two.

Time has thinned the royal courts of Europe and the surviving available princesses, for one reason or another, merit hardly a second glance. Denmark's Princess Anne-Marie, for a long time a firm favourite with would-be prophets, is now out of the running. The young King Constantine of Greece made sure of her as his queen while she was not yet out of her teens. Of those who remain it seems doubtful if any can measure up to the exacting three-fold conditions required for Britain's future queen.

Let us examine these conditions briefly. On the purely personal side it is not unreasonable to assume that whoever Prince Charles eventually marries, it will be someone who appeals to him (and, presumably, he in turn must appeal to her). Genetically, a close degree of consanguinity would seem inadvisable, which possibly rules out the daughters of Prince Philip's sisters. Regally, the girl of his choice must be acceptable to both his own Royal Family and to the British Parliament and people.

If the possibility of a royal bride from Europe can be largely discarded, what then remains? Suggestions that Britain's future queen may perhaps hail from one of the lusty, young nations of the Commonwealth, heart-stirring though they are, would seem hardly able to stand the test of closer examination. The personal side of love and courtship demands more than a casual meeting or a passing acquaintanceship. It requires proximity and the passage of time . . . closer proximity and a longer passage of time than Prince Charles is likely to find at his disposal on such Commonwealth visits as may come his way in the future. Yet the possibility cannot be entirely ruled out.

But the real likelihood remains that he will find his future bride in his own country, though even here his freedom of choice is likely to be restricted. His Aunt Margo—Princess Margaret— may have married a photographer, but she was not the heir to the Throne. Prince Charles, as the future King, is unlikely to have the same freedom of choice. While his marriage may not be an arranged one in the sense in which such things were once contrived (and still are in some countries), there will almost certainly be gentle urgings in some directions and tactful intervention in others.

All things considered, the odds are that his bride will come, as his grandfather's did before him, from the small, aristocratic circle of royal friends and acquaintances. Of course, nothing—as a previous Prince of Wales has shown—can be completely ruled out. But the probability remains, and if the result is to give Britain and the Commonwealth a future queen cast in the same sensible, dutiful, hard-working, essentially charming mould as the woman who is now the Queen Mother, then few will quarrel with his choice.

It has been said that the qualities required of a king in this modern age are that he should be neither too forceful nor too intellectual, but a middle-of-the-road man capable of being all things to all people. If this is true, let us consider how far Prince Charles fills the bill.

In him, there would seem to be no extremes of character. He has, as far as can be assessed, inherited neither his father's occasional arrogance nor his maternal grandfather's famous temper. If he shows few indications of his father's powers of drive and leadership, these are perhaps qualities better suited to a consort than a monarch. In their stead, Prince Charles has patience and understanding, imagination and a love of artistic things. If he lacks Prince Philip's gift for witty repartee, he has inherited his mother's thoughtfulness together with a deep sense of duty which stems from both parents. He has grit, determination and a growing self-confidence. He has the benefit of a warm, close-knit family life and a father's example of how royal life can be lived.

Prince Philip, when he married the young woman who is now the Queen, could very easily have settled for a lotus-eating life which would have made him no more than a shadow of his wife. But that was neither his nature nor his way. While never once usurping the Queen's traditional right to the main spotlight on the royal stage, he has yet contrived for himself a supporting role of substance and strength which has, if anything, enhanced the Queen's own position.

With his father's example before him, there seems no reason why the youthful Prince of Wales should not do the same, finding, as Prince Philip has found, a life of rich purpose in the wings as he awaits that future day when the trumpets shrill and the heralds proclaim him . . .

His Most Excellent Majesty King Charles III.